ESSENTIALS OF

Discursive Psychology

Essentials of Qualitative Methods Series

Essentials of Autoethnography
 Christopher N. Poulos

Essentials of Consensual Qualitative Research
 Clara E. Hill and Sarah Knox

Essentials of Descriptive-Interpretive Qualitative Research: A Generic Approach
 Robert Elliott and Ladislav Timulak

Essentials of Discursive Psychology
 Linda M. McMullen

ESSENTIALS OF

Discursive Psychology

Linda M. McMullen

 AMERICAN PSYCHOLOGICAL ASSOCIATION

The opinions and statements published are the responsibility of the author, and such opinions and statements do not necessarily represent the policies of the American Psychological Association.

Published by
American Psychological Association
750 First Street, NE
Washington, DC 20002
https://www.apa.org

Order Department
https://www.apa.org/pubs/books
order@apa.org

In the U.K., Europe, Africa, and the Middle East, copies may be ordered from Eurospan
https://www.eurospanbookstore.com/apa
info@eurospangroup.com

Typeset in Charter by Circle Graphics, Inc., Reisterstown, MD

Printer: Sheridan Books, Chelsea, MI
Cover Designer: Anne Kerns, Anne Likes Red, Silver Spring, MD

Library of Congress Cataloging-in-Publication Data

Names: McMullen, Linda M., author.
Title: Essentials of discursive psychology / Linda M. McMullen.
Description: Washington, DC : American Psychological Association, [2021] |
  Series: Essentials of qualitative methods | Includes bibliographical references
  and index.
Identifiers: LCCN 2020026757 (print) | LCCN 2020026758 (ebook) |
  ISBN 9781433834639 (paperback) | ISBN 9781433834646 (ebook)
Subjects: LCSH: Discursive psychology.
Classification: LCC BF201.3 .M36 2021 (print) | LCC BF201.3 (ebook) |
  DDC 150.72/1—dc23
LC record available at https://lccn.loc.gov/2020026757
LC ebook record available at https://lccn.loc.gov/2020026758

https://doi.org/10.1037/0000220-000

Printed in the United States of America

10 9 8 7 6 5 4 3 2 1

Contents

Series Foreword—Clara E. Hill and Sarah Knox   *vii*

1. **Conceptual Foundations of Discursive Psychology**   **3**
   What Is Discourse, and What Is Discourse Analysis?   *4*
   What Is Discursive Psychology, and What Is Critical Discursive Psychology?   *5*
   Why Choose Discursive Psychology, and What Does This Choice Entail?   *6*
   What Are Some Major Components of Discursive Psychology?   *10*
   Deciding Whether to Use This Methodology   *13*

2. **Designing a Study**   **15**
   Stating the Topic and Engaging in Initial Searches of Literatures   *15*
   Framing the Research Question(s)   *17*
   *Determining What Type of Data to Collect or Generate to Address Your
   Research Questions*   *21*

3. **Collecting and Generating Data**   **27**
   Collecting Archival or Already Existing Data   *28*
   Generating Data From Interviews or Focus Groups   *29*

4. **Analyzing Your Data**   **35**
   A Process of Data Analysis   *35*
   Examples of Detailed Analyses of Extracts of Data   *40*
   Concluding Comments on Analyzing Your Data   *64*

5. **Disseminating Your Research**   **67**

   Preparing a Manuscript for Publication in a Journal   *67*

   Beyond the Manuscript   *72*

6. **What Constitutes Good Discursive Research?**   **73**

   Documentation   *74*

   Demonstration   *74*

   Plausibility   *75*

   Coherence   *76*

   Fruitfulness   *76*

7. **Ongoing Conversations**   **79**

   Questions of Ethics   *79*

   Questions Related to Conceptual Advancements and Methodological Innovations   *83*

   Final Thoughts   *84*

Appendix A: Exemplar Studies   *85*

Appendix B: Commonly Used Transcription Notations   *87*

Appendix C: Examples of Discursive Devices and Resources   *89*

References   *93*

Index   *101*

About the Author   *107*

About the Series Editors   *109*

Series Foreword

Qualitative approaches have become accepted and indeed embraced as empirical methods within the social sciences, as scholars have realized that many of the phenomena in which we are interested are complex and require deep inner reflection and equally penetrating examination. Quantitative approaches often cannot capture such phenomena well through their standard methods (e.g., self-report measures), so qualitative designs using interviews and other in-depth data-gathering procedures offer exciting, nimble, and useful research approaches.

Indeed, the number and variety of qualitative approaches that have been developed is remarkable. We remember Bill Stiles saying (quoting Chairman Mao) at one meeting about methods, "Let a hundred flowers bloom," indicating that there are many appropriate methods for addressing research questions. In this series, we celebrate this diversity (hence, the cover design of flowers).

The question for many of us, though, has been how to decide among approaches and how to learn the different methods. Many prior descriptions of the various qualitative methods have not provided clear enough descriptions of the methods, making it difficult for novice researchers to learn how to use them. Thus, those interested in learning about and pursuing qualitative research need crisp and thorough descriptions of these approaches, with lots of examples to illustrate the method so that readers can grasp how to use the methods.

The purpose of this series of books, then, is to present a range of different qualitative approaches that seemed most exciting and illustrative of the range of methods appropriate for social science research. We asked leading experts in qualitative methods to contribute to the series, and we were delighted that they accepted our invitation. Through this series, readers have the opportunity to learn qualitative research methods from those who developed the methods and/or who have been using them successfully for years.

We asked the authors of each book to provide context for the method, including a rationale, situating the method within the qualitative tradition, describing the method's philosophical and epistemological background, and noting the key features of the method. We then asked them to describe in detail the steps of the method, including the research team, sampling, biases and expectations, data collection, data analysis, and variations on the method. We also asked authors to provide tips for the research process and for writing a manuscript emerging from a study that used the method. Finally, we asked authors to reflect on the methodological integrity of the approach, along with the benefits and limitations of the particular method.

This series of books can be used in several different ways. Instructors teaching courses in qualitative research could use the whole series, presenting one method at a time as they expose students to a range of qualitative methods. Alternatively, instructors could choose to focus on just a few approaches, as depicted in specific books, supplementing the books with examples from studies that have been published using the approaches, and providing experiential exercises to help students get started using the approaches.

In this book, Linda M. McMullen guides readers through the fundamentals of discursive psychology. Discursive psychology involves analysis and interpretation of written or spoken language. Given that our communications are laden with social messages and constitutive of social actions, the study of language can reveal much about relationships and culture. As Dr. McMullen shows us, discursive psychology provides a clear, coherent approach for analyzing talk and text and for situating discourse within social contexts.

—*Clara E. Hill and Sarah Knox*

ESSENTIALS OF

Discursive Psychology

1 CONCEPTUAL FOUNDATIONS OF DISCURSIVE PSYCHOLOGY

All of us are discourse analysts in our everyday lives. We listen to others speak, we read texts, and we make meaning of, and interpret, what is said or written. We also attend to how something is said or written and can understand the same word, phrase, or sentence in different ways depending on the speaker's or writer's tone. What sets discursive analysis as a qualitative research methodology apart from these everyday activities is the analyst's deliberate showing of what it is in the speaker's or writer's use of language that results in particular understandings and interpretations of what is said or written.

In this book, I provide a brief introduction to (a) the philosophical and theoretical assumptions of discursive psychology; (b) considerations involved in designing a discursive study, including the kinds of questions that are suitably addressed via this form of research and the types of data that can be collected or generated to address them; (c) how to engage in an analysis of data using this methodological perspective, including various analytic strategies that can be used and the types of linguistic resources and devices that are available to speakers and writers who use the English language; (d) how to communicate and assess such research; and (e) ongoing

https://doi.org/10.1037/0000220-001
Essentials of Discursive Psychology, by L. M. McMullen

conversations about ethical, conceptual, and methodological issues related to discursive psychology. Let us begin with a few definitions.

WHAT IS DISCOURSE, AND WHAT IS DISCOURSE ANALYSIS?

Discourse can be straightforwardly defined as spoken or written communication. It follows, then, that the term *discourse analysis* can be understood as the analysis of such communication. However, in the context of research, discourse analysis is a nonspecific term. It has been used to refer to (a) a *method* or set of strategies or procedures for analyzing data that have been collected or generated to address particular research questions; (b) a *methodology* or plan of action that underlies our choice of particular methods of data analysis and links this choice to what the researcher hopes to achieve with the research (Crotty, 1998, p. 3); (c) a perspective on social life that includes metatheoretical and theoretical, along with analytic, principles; and (d) a critique of cognitivism in psychology (Potter, 2003; Willig, 2001; Wood & Kroger, 2000)—that is, of the notion that cognitive processes are the primary shapers of human action (Edwards & Potter, 1992).

Furthermore, when used to refer to a research methodology, discourse analysis is best thought of as an umbrella term that covers many different forms of analysis with different foci and goals and that demands further specification. Discourse analysis has been used, for example, to refer to a focus on

- how sentences are put together (linguistics),

- how conversation or talk-in-interaction is structured (conversation analysis),

- how objects and subjects are constituted in language (Foucauldian discourse analysis), and

- how patterns of language use can be understood in relation to the exercising of power in social relationships (critical discourse analysis; McMullen, 2011, p. 205; see Wiggins, 2017, Chapter 2, for a more comprehensive overview of various forms of discourse analysis).

So, although discourse analysis is rightfully understood as a major form of qualitative research now undertaken by psychologists, it is imperative that you specify what form (or combination of forms) of discourse analysis you are using and why.

WHAT IS DISCURSIVE PSYCHOLOGY, AND WHAT IS CRITICAL DISCURSIVE PSYCHOLOGY?

Further specification of discourse analysis has also occurred in relation to its application to questions of psychological relevance. The first articulation of what is sometimes referred to as discursive social psychology (Potter, 1998), discourse analysis in social psychology (Wood & Kroger, 2000), or eventually, discursive psychology, as popularized in the United Kingdom (Edwards & Potter, 1992), was by Potter and Wetherell (1987). As part of the "turn to language" that occurred in the 1980s in the social sciences, in general, and psychology, in particular, Potter and Wetherell promoted the analysis of talk and text as an important focus in and of itself, rather than as a route to inner cognitive processes.

In addition to foregrounding this theoretical perspective on language, discursive psychology has come to be associated with evolving analytic foci. In what Potter (2012) called "strand one" of discursive psychology, the focus is on identifying the interpretative repertoires or conceptually organized clusters of terms, phrases, grammatical features, and figures of speech that are used to build social action and, often, to maintain existing configurations of power and inequality. "Strand two" of discursive psychology, according to Potter, is focused on what speakers and writers are doing with language—on the social actions that are being performed. Are speakers, for example, arguing, assuming blame, complimenting, belittling, demanding, or acquiescing? As emphasized by Wiggins (2017), this strand is also concerned with a reenvisioning of psychological concepts, such as attitudes, beliefs, and emotions, as "socially managed" (p. 4). That is, rather than being located "within" the person, these concepts are understood as social practices that transpire between people, often in conversation or other verbal exchanges. For example, advocating for the legalization of cannabis would be understood not as an indication of a speaker holding a liberal attitude; rather, it would be seen as a social action that was performed in a particular context with particular interactional consequences. "Strand three" of discursive psychology was characterized by Potter as involving close attention to the sequential structure of talk that is typical of conversation analysis. The focus of this strand is on what are often considered the micro features of interaction, including, for example, grammatical forms, pauses, intonation, and turn taking.

Critical discursive psychology has grown out of Wetherell's (1998) contention that the focus on showing what people are doing with language in talk and/or text, along with the interactional consequences of this doing, should be combined with a focus on the broader normative conceptions—or ways of understanding and being in the world—that are associated with the historical, social, and cultural contexts in which such talk and text are located. So, for example, talk or text about legalizing cannabis might be understood in relation to broader culturally and historically available discourses or ways of talking or writing about the topic of cannabis use. In Canada, where cannabis is legal, such discourses might include a focus on the continued need for deterrence through criminalization, the potential health benefits of legalization, or the freeing up of the criminal justice system from unnecessary prosecution of cannabis users. So, this approach takes seriously the notion that speakers and writers exist in worlds populated with discourses—or particular ways of speaking and writing—which can both enable and constrain how they speak and write. Sometimes referred to as a synthetic approach, this form of discursive psychology takes the more detailed analysis of talk and text afforded by discursive psychology and connects it to broader patterns of speaking and writing that are available to language users by their cultural and historical location.

This book focuses on showing how attention to these micro and macro levels of analysis of discursively oriented questions of psychological relevance can be used to investigate topics of interest to social scientists. I have chosen to focus on this approach to discourse analysis because of its connection with the discipline of psychology and because it requires a reconceptualization of language and its uses that can be useful in understanding other approaches to discourse analysis. My use of the term *discursive psychology* should be understood, however, in a broad sense. Specifically, this book does not focus exclusively on a particular strand of discursive psychology or critical discursive psychology as they are defined and demarcated by Potter (2012) and Wiggins (2017). Rather, I draw on examples from my research and from the research literature that sometimes display a fairly detailed analysis of an extract of talk or text or that sometimes combine this sort of analysis with attention to the broader discursive context(s)—culturally and historically available discourses, in which the sequences of talk or text are located. But why might you choose to use such an approach? What is afforded, and what is challenged by such a choice?

WHY CHOOSE DISCURSIVE PSYCHOLOGY, AND WHAT DOES THIS CHOICE ENTAIL?

Put simply, discursive psychology allows you to address questions about how people, located in particular contexts of time and space, take up available discourses and use features of language (sometimes referred to as linguistic devices, strategies, or resources) to perform social actions, including how they construct versions of reality with what possible consequences. For example, this approach would be useful if you were interested in how people use scientific discourses to argue for and against the notion of human-induced climate change, in how they justify their decision to start vaping, or in how they criticize each other in face-to-face encounters. However, of all the qualitative methodologies used by psychologists, discursive psychology ranks among the most challenging. In part, as we will see later, these challenges have to do with learning how to use this methodology—for example, how to become familiar with a wide-ranging set of linguistic resources, how to use a set of analytic strategies that focus on both micro and macro levels of analysis, and how to use one's familiarity (or lack thereof) with local customs or norms in making interpretations as to what is going on in talk or text. But, perhaps even more challenging is how discursive psychology upends many of the taken-for-granted notions in the discipline of psychology as it has traditionally been framed and practiced in the United States and Canada.

Let us touch briefly on how discursive psychology departs from some of these taken-for-granted notions.

Epistemology

Discursive psychology is not grounded in an objectivist epistemology, the theory of knowledge that maintains that "meaning, and therefore meaningful reality, exists . . . apart from the operation of any consciousness" (Crotty, 1998, p. 8). That is, it does not adhere to the notion that meaning resides in objects themselves and that human beings can discover (or come close to discovering) objective truths. Instead, much of the research that is conducted with this approach proceeds from a constructionist epistemology or theory of knowledge. Crotty (1998) defined *constructionism* as "the view that *all knowledge, and therefore all meaningful reality as such, is contingent upon human practices, being constructed in and out of interaction between human beings and their world, and developed and transmitted within an essentially social context*" (p. 42; italics in original). So, in contrast to objectivism, constructionism is based on the premise that there is no meaning without a human mind and that meaning is constructed in the interactions between human beings and their world(s). If meaning comes into being in this fashion, then language—a primary means by which human beings communicate and interact—is at the heart of meaning making. In addition, because the worlds with which human beings are interacting are not fixed, but ever changing, it follows that, as Burr (1995) stated, "the ways in which we commonly understand [these worlds], the categories and concepts we use, are historically and culturally specific" (p. 3). A discursive psychologist interested in studying a category or concept such as "depression" or "gender identity," for example, would understand it as having been brought into being in particular historical–cultural locations, as having greater resonance in some locations than in others, and as continuing to change as people rework it in their interactions with each other.

Theoretical Perspective

Discursive psychology does not proceed from the perspective of post-positivism, that scientific "truths" are provisional statements, which, due to the limits that human senses impose on our ability to observe reality and to the changing nature of what it is we are observing, we know with a level of probability, but not with certainty (Crotty, 1998). Rather, it is compatible with a variety of non-postpositivist theoretical perspectives, including, as Crotty (1998) noted, various forms of critical theory and inquiry (p. 5). With its location in constructionism, discursive psychology assumes a critical stance toward taken-for-granted knowledge (Burr, 1995), which often involves a questioning of the very categories we assume to be "givens" and a sensitivity to how these categories structure our worlds and with what possible consequences. Although adherents to this approach typically do not deny the existence of a material world—they can assume realism in ontology (the study of being)—they contend that what we think of as realities are made meaningful only through the use of ever-changing historically and culturally constituted discourses or patterns of language. So, all of what we know is contextually situated and subject to change. For example, consider how our language with respect to gender and sexual identity has moved in many parts of the world from male or female and homosexual or heterosexual to include lesbian, gay, bisexual, transgender, cisgender, transsexual, queer, two-spirit, to name a few.

Process of Knowledge Production

Discursive psychology is not based on the hypothetico-deductive method. It does not attempt to falsify propositions (hypotheses) that are deduced from scientific theories, as is often the case in experimental (or quasi-experimental) research. Instead, discursive psychology is guided by research questions and relies on a process of drawing out, articulating, and interpreting patterns in the data that are relevant to these questions. On occasion, the development of these questions might be guided by theory, but more often than not, they are derived from your observations and wonderings about practices in everyday life. Typically, questions are constituted in terms of "what" (as in "What discursive resources are brought to bear as speakers or writers construct particular versions of events?") and "how" (as in "How is a particular social action performed?") and are sensitive to the context(s) in which they are asked.

Goal

Discursive psychology does not seek to explain and predict. Its goal is not to develop models that show how variables interrelate, possibly in cause–effect manners. Although the pursuit of factors–outcomes relations is eschewed, discursive psychologists can address "why" questions if speakers or writers orient to constructing causal relations. For example, if a writer of a newspaper article on increasing levels of anxiety being reported by millennials referred to concerns about climate change, precarious work, and high costs of housing as reasons for rising anxiety, you would be able to claim that the writer is invoking this causal link. Regardless of the question posed in this approach to discursive research, however, the task of showing and interpreting, of linking evidence in the talk and text to analytic claims about what is transpiring and being achieved in the talk or text, is taken as a goal in and of itself.

Cognitivism

Discursive psychology is not based in cognitivist approaches that seek to "theorise, examine, and measure mental processes" (Wiggins, 2017, p. 28) and which "[interpret] people's talk and behaviours primarily in terms of underlying cognitive causes" (p. 242). In particular, as articulated by Willig (2001), it challenges taken-for-granted notions that talk is a route to cognitions, that we can get at what people are thinking by analyzing what they are saying and that relatively enduring cognitive structures, such as beliefs and attitudes, exist. Discursive psychology privileges the production of talk and text as being situated in a social context (Potter, 2003). So, rather than talk and text being understood as routes to relatively enduring cognitive structures held by speakers and writers, talking and writing are understood as practices that are oriented to the context in which their production occurs and, therefore, as relative. For example, a person's advocating for medical assistance in dying would be understood not as the person's enduring belief. Rather, it would be analyzed and interpreted as a discursive move that occurs in a particular context, accomplishes particular interactional business between persons, and has particular consequences in the context in which it occurred.

Focus

Discursive psychology is not an analysis of the person. In contrast to the interests and activities of much of the discipline of psychology, it does not seek to interpret and theorize people's thoughts, feelings, experiences, and behaviors either at the level of the individual or the group. Instead, the focus of analysis in discursive psychology is on how language is being used in talk and text, not on what these uses have to say about characteristics of individual persons (speakers or writers). This reorientation away from individual persons and how their use of language tells us something about their personhood is often a difficult shift for psychology students because it goes against our disciplinary focus. However, it is an essential feature of the analyst's orientation in discursive psychology.

WHAT ARE SOME MAJOR COMPONENTS OF DISCURSIVE PSYCHOLOGY?

I revisit the assumptions and principles of discursive psychology throughout this book, but it might be useful to highlight a few key notions to keep in mind as you engage with this methodology.

Conceptions of Language Use

Potter (2003) articulated three theoretical principles of discursive analysis that should help you think of the use of language in ways that might not readily come to mind. First, this form of analysis focuses on the action orientation of discourse, on how speakers and writers use discursive resources and with what effects. So, rather than theorizing language as a way of communicating or representing our perceptions of objects and events in the world, it relies on a conception of language as performative, as outlined by Austin (1962) in his speech act theory. This emphasis on action—on what utterances do (see Potter, 2003)—places the focus of analysis on how people use discursive devices and resources, such as particular words, sentence structures, paralinguistic features (e.g., intonation, emphases, pitch), and broader discourses or framings of objects and events in the world, to perform social actions. So, rather than focusing exclusively or primarily on the content of what people are saying or writing, the emphasis is on what the talk or text is achieving in the specific context in which it occurs. For example, depending on the context, an utterance such as "It's raining today" might be taken as a suggestion or command to take one's umbrella rather than as a declarative statement about the weather conditions of the day.

Second, discursive psychology is based on the notion of discourse as situated. Specifically, discourse is understood as being organized sequentially at the level of the sentence, that words are put together in various orders and that such orderings can matter. Consider, for example, the difference in meaning between "I want only the best for you" and "I want the best only for you." Discourse is also understood as being organized sequentially via sentences—sentences are connected in that what is said typically follows from what was just said and sets up what is said next. So, how a hearer responds to an utterance can tell you something about the effects of the utterance on the hearer. For example, consider the following sequence:

SPEAKER A: The garbage is smelly.

SPEAKER B: Okay, I'll take it out right away.

SPEAKER A: Thank you.

In this example, a structurally declarative utterance by Speaker A is taken as a call for action by Speaker B, which, in turn, is received with an appreciation token by Speaker A. Discourse is also understood as being situated contextually. That is, what is said or written and how it is said or written depends on contextual features such as who is speaking, who is the audience, the setting, and the purpose of the talk or text. For example, a person might put together one version of a weekend's events when talking with friends and another when talking with one's boss.

Third, there is an emphasis on talk and text as constructed—as being built from various discursive resources—and as constructive—as producing various versions of persons, events, actions, worlds. That is, speakers and writers have access to a range of resources, such as words and phrases that can be used literally or metaphorically, paralinguistic features (e.g., intonation, pitch, emphases), nonlexical sounds (e.g., sighing, laughing), and silences and pauses that are typically used in combination to produce particular renderings of persons and accounts of events, practices, actions, and worlds. Keeping your focus on these conceptions of language use— on the performative aspects of language, the situatedness of discourse, the discursive devices and resources available to speakers and writers, and what is produced with these devices and resources—should assist you in adopting a mindset that enables you to conduct discursive analysis.

Centrality of Context

Context and how it is intricately implicated in what you will produce from engaging in discursive psychology must be notions to which you constantly return. From the moment you decide that a discursive study is appropriate for the kinds of research questions you want to ask about your topic, to the articulation of your research questions, to the design of your study (including what will constitute the talk and text you are going to analyze to address your research questions), and to the analysis and interpretation of your data, you should repeatedly be asking yourself how you understand the context(s) of your study and the possible ways these contexts are shaping your data and your analyses. Doing so should help you keep in mind that you are tapping into historically and culturally available ways of speaking and writing, that data and analytic interpretations are always generated in a particular context (or in particular contexts), and that all knowledge is situated and provisional. For example, choosing to use data generated from research interviews is likely to produce different analytic yields than choosing to use data available in online forums.

Versions and Accounts

The centrality of context, along with the theoretical principles of language use articulated by Potter (2003) and summarized earlier, underscore the point that, as discursive analysts, we are dealing with accounts produced by speakers and writers—versions of events, actions, and features of worlds that vary with the context(s) in which they are constructed. This notion applies to what is produced by you, the analyst, as well. In other words, there is no one (or certainly correct) way to analyze talk and text. Different analysts will produce different versions of an analysis, along with different interpretations, even from the same data and with the same set of research questions. Analysts, of course, have a stake in the believability of their analysis from a reader's perspective, so it is not the case that "anything goes" in this kind of work. However, when engaging in discursive analysis, you will have to become (at least reasonably) comfortable with the notion that there is no right or true answer to your research question(s).

Careful Linking of Evidence to Analytic Claims and Interpretations

Discursive analysis is difficult work. As we will see later, it requires you to (a) repeatedly engage with your data, (b) make decisions about what in your data addresses your research questions, and (c) repeatedly delve into your selections of data. In addition, it demands that you link evidence to your analytic claims and your interpretations. This evidence is usually in the form of specific discursive devices and resources, including broader historical, cultural, or societal discourses relied on by speakers and writers. Your analytic claims are often about the business that is being done via the use of these devices and resources, whereas your interpretations typically speak to what possible functions are being served by the use of these devices and resources, along with possible consequences. Although this work is often painstaking, its outcomes can be stimulating, revelatory, and even emancipating.

DECIDING WHETHER TO USE THIS METHODOLOGY

Given what is now a vast array of qualitative methodologies that are available for use by researchers with an interest in questions of psychological relevance, how will you decide whether discursive psychology is suitable and appropriate for your research interests and goals? Although I always tell students that, in theory, their research questions—what they are interested in learning about their topic or substantive area of interest— should drive their choice of methodology, more often than not, researchers' familiarity and comfort with a particular methodology begin to shape how they think about their topic and, subsequently, their research questions and choice of methodology. So, an understanding of social life and conceptions of talk and text in the way I have presented it does not typically develop on its own; rather, it is shaped over time by your experiences of engaging with the principles and practices of discursive psychology. So, there is a dynamic interplay between how you understand what you intend to research, your familiarity with existing methodologies, and your choice of methodology. However, if you understand social life to be propelled by how people use language, and if you conceive of talk and text as actively constructed versions of aspects of social life and features of the world, this approach might be a methodology of choice for your research.

As the first step in deciding whether to engage in discursive psychology, I recommend that you read articles based on this methodology. I provide a list of examples of such articles in Appendix A. Reading these articles (and others) will enable you to begin the process of familiarizing yourself with the kinds of discursive devices and resources that researchers attend to and how they make analytic claims about what speakers and writers are doing with these devices and resources. You will then be in a better position to decide whether this kind of work suits your research interests and your particular analytic preferences.

2 DESIGNING A STUDY

By the time you have decided that taking a discursive approach is appropriate for your research interests, you will already have a sense of the broad focus of these interests. You now have to consider more particularly how you can design a discursive study that addresses these interests. In this chapter, I explore how you can begin to shape your particular research project, including formulating a topic statement, engaging with initial searches of various literatures, stating your research questions, and deciding which kinds of data can address these questions.

STATING THE TOPIC AND ENGAGING IN INITIAL SEARCHES OF LITERATURES

As is often the case with qualitative inquiry, what you are interested in learning about—the topic of your research—is typically something that intrigues or excites you. Perhaps you have become fascinated by what you observe to be changing conceptions of marriage and wedding ceremonies in contemporary life, what appears to be a rise in the frequency with which

https://doi.org/10.1037/0000220-002
Essentials of Discursive Psychology, by L. M. McMullen

celebrities and other prominent figures make public apologies, or what the availability of medical assistance in dying means for people's end-of-life decision making. A first step in determining whether to carry out research on any of these topics might be to engage in reflexivity, a process by which you reflect on how you came to be intrigued by the topic, what about the topic interests you, and what you presently sense as your knowledge about the topic. These reflections are usually documented in a written format but could be generated via auditory or visual modes (e.g., audio recordings, drawings). In contrast with most other qualitative methodologies, however, reflexivity in discursive research (if it occurs at all) is not taken to be an indicator of transparency in the service of quality control. Rather, it can be a useful way for you to understand how your initial topic statement and subsequently fashioned research questions have taken shape over the course of your research project and to remind yourself of the salience of context in discursive research.

In conjunction with an opening statement of your topic of interest, you can begin what will be a series of forays into the literatures on your topic. I pluralize literature because you should consult a range of sources to clarify your thinking on your topic. Although searching the typical psychology databases is perhaps a place to start, it is not unusual to find that they sometimes yield little of relevance. I always encourage my students to do a wide-ranging search of literatures from other disciplines, including, to name only a few, anthropology, sociology, health sciences, linguistics, communications, media studies, humanities, public policy, and justice studies. Both quantitative and qualitative studies can inform your topic statement, and it is important not to foreclose on the potential usefulness of a study on the basis of its methodology. However, with the increasing use of qualitative methodologies in many disciplines, a sizable number of journals are now dedicated solely to qualitative research (e.g., *Qualitative Health Research, Qualitative Psychology, Qualitative Research, Qualitative Research in Psychology*) and to discursive research (e.g., *Discourse & Society, Discourse Studies*), and these journals should be specifically targeted for perusal. I also suggest that my students look for any relevant gray literature—for example, newspaper articles, magazines, pamphlets, websites, blogs, popular books, unpublished dissertations and theses—and go beyond written sources to search visual (e.g., drawings, graffiti, posters), auditory (e.g., music), and mixed sources (e.g., movies). Although such sources do not have the same status as peer-reviewed publications, they can, nevertheless, inform you about the cultural currency of your topic or aspects of it. I recognize that the inclusiveness of such a search strategy can seem overwhelming. However, it is important to remember that the process is iterative; you can continue to search various sources for relevant material even up to the point of data analysis and interpretation.

FRAMING THE RESEARCH QUESTION(S)

After you have developed an initial topic statement ("I'm interested in studying . . .") and conducted some initial searches of literatures, you should begin to frame your research questions. Remember, of course, that topic statements and research questions are not cast in stone and that it is possible that your focus will be slightly or even considerably altered once you have collected or generated your data. That is, you might find something intriguing or unexpected in your data that results in a restatement of the topic and/or research question(s).

As I noted in the previous chapter, research questions within the context of this approach are typically framed in "how" or "what" terms. If your interest is in the business that is being performed via talk or text, it can be useful to think in "how" terms. In this case, your focus might be on how (and the various ways in which) a particular social action (e.g., apologizing, agreeing, criticizing, disputing) is carried out. For example, if you were interested in controversies about the use of antidepressants, you might ask, "How is criticism of a decision to use (or not use) an antidepressant managed in online forums?" If you are interested in the particular features of talk or text—the linguistic devices that people use in fashioning their accounts—with the subject positions that speakers or writers adopt for themselves or assign to others, or with the broader societal discourses from which speakers or writers draw in fashioning their talk or text, it might be useful to think in "what" terms. In this case, your focus might be on identifying these devices, resources, subject positions, or societal discourses and the functions they serve in particular talk or text. For example, with respect to the topic of controversies in the use of antidepressants, you might ask, "What functions are served by invoking etiological discourses of depression in online forums?"

Here, I have separated these two categories of questions to emphasize the importance of structuring your research questions in these terms. Most often, however, these two categories merge. Research questions that are framed in "how" terms often encompass an analysis of the "what," and similarly, "what" questions can also include an analysis of "how" devices, resources, positions, and discourses are used. For example, in an interview-based study on discontinuing antidepressants, Jennifer Herman and I asked the question "How do women fashion accounts of their decisions to quit taking antidepressants without their doctors' permission?" (McMullen & Herman, 2009). To address this question, we focused on the work that was being performed by the interviewees in their talk and how the interviewees positioned themselves and others—how selves and others were constituted via discursive practices (Davies & Harré, 1990) that were used during the interviews. We identified three discursive strategies used by the interviewees in fashioning their accounts of deciding to discontinue antidepressants: (a) referencing actual or potential (often negative) effects of antidepressants, (b) resisting medical knowledge by positioning one's own or others' (lay) knowledge as superior, and (c) denigrating medical authorities. These discursive strategies constituted (some of) the actions performed by the interviewees (i.e., how they justified their decisions). We then focused on how the interviewees were constituting themselves and others (the what) and showed how the use of these strategies was linked to the interviewees positioning themselves as responsible and, on occasion, others as irresponsible. In this example, our research question was framed in "how" terms and easily enabled us to address "what" and "how" in our analysis.

Similarly, a focus on what appears to be the "what" can also include an analysis of the "how." In a study of "ordinary" citizens' talk of issues surrounding domestic water and energy consumption, Kurz et al. (2005) framed the goal of their research as "to identify the ways in which energy and water are constructed as resources and the discursive strategies mobilized by members of one particular community to account for and legitimize specific resource-consumption practices" (p. 606). Their analysis of interview data focused on, for example, the construction of water as a "precious commodity" (p. 607) and energy as "technology" (p. 610) but also on how the discursive strategy of subject positioning was used by speakers to position themselves as "concerned" and others as "careless" (p. 613) and responsible for wasting resources. In this case, the goal of identifying ways and strategies (the what) easily accommodated an analysis of how constructions of water and energy were used in conjunction with subject positionings.

In a study on children's talk about parental mental disorder, Alasuutari and Järvi (2012) explicitly framed their research question as focusing on both the "what" and the "how." Specifically, they asked, "What are the discourses (vocabularies) that children affected by parental mental disorder use as their resources when they talk about a parent's mental disorder?" (p. 134) and "How are the parental problems talked about and accounted for in the interviewer–child interaction?" (p. 136). Their analysis focused on presenting the broad contours of three discourses (or vocabularies)—professional, empirical, and concern (the what)—and on showing how these discourses were invoked in the interactions between the interviewer and the children and with what possible functions and consequences. Phrasing their research question with this dual focus enabled these researchers to focus on both the macro level—the broader discourses or patterns of speaking that were available to the research participants and on which they drew—and the micro level—the interactional instantiations of the use of these discourses.

Is it possible to address why questions via discursive psychology? Although this methodology is not used to investigate cause–effect or factor–outcome relations as is done in objectivist, quantitative research, it is possible that a discursive analyst might be interested in how people fashion explanations related to a particular topic. However, these explanations would be understood as accounts or versions or ways of making sense of events or happenings in the world and would be evaluated not in terms of their truth status but with respect to their possible functions and consequences. So, although discursive psychology does not address why questions in an attempt to establish causality, speakers' and writers' explanatory accounts are sometimes of interest to discursive researchers.

Are there any limits to the content of questions that can be investigated via discursive psychology? Although this methodology was originally focused on a reconceptualizing of central psychological concepts such as attitudes, beliefs, cognitions, and emotions, researchers have subsequently used it to investigate a wide range of topics of importance to human life. For example, discursive psychology has been used to study how seemingly everyday practices (e.g., marriage; Lawes, 1999) and contemporary issues (e.g., climate change; Kurz et al., 2010) are constructed, how social actions (e.g., apology; McNeill et al., 2014) are performed, how a particular figure of speech (e.g., the depression–diabetes analogy; McMullen & Sigurdson, 2014) is invoked, how identity positions (e.g., motherhood and fatherhood; Alexander & McMullen, 2015) are fashioned in discourse, and how discourses (e.g., racism; Wetherell & Potter, 1993) are constituted.

Although the range of topics and foci suitable for investigation with this approach has expanded, there is evidence that how researchers are fashioning their research questions is becoming more specific and contextualized. For example, Goodman and Burke (2010) asked how members of the British public talk about the racist, or not racist, nature of opposing asylum seeking (p. 327). In doing so, the authors signaled the specificity and limits of who provided data for their study (members of the British public) and in what context (talk of opposing asylum seeking). Similarly,

Kurz et al. (2010) stated that their interest was in the "various ways in which the issue of climate change was invoked and rhetorically managed by each of the two major parties in the lead up to the [Australian] election" (p. 601). In this case, readers are oriented to particular speakers (politicians from the two major political parties), a particular time (prelude to an election), and a particular context (Australia). In an even more precisely framed question, Lawless et al. (2018) asked how information about dementia risk prevention is presented on websites of the most prominent English-language, nonprofit dementia organizations (p. 1539). Here, we see particularities about the topic (information about dementia risk prevention) coupled with significant detail about the source of data generation (websites of prominent English-language, nonprofit dementia organizations). These specificities in research questions signal that discursive researchers take seriously that (a) who is speaking or writing, (b) to whom, (c) about what, and (d) in what context shapes what is enacted and produced and how it is enacted and produced. Drawing attention to the significance of context in stating your research question(s) reinforces the imperative to foreground context from the beginning and throughout your project.

One final word on framing one's research question(s): Although it might appear from what I have said that one moves rather seamlessly from the selection of a topic to articulating one's question(s), it is not infrequently the case that the final form of your question(s) will be forged during and perhaps even on completion of your analysis. That is, you might begin with a rather general question (or with general questions) and then particularize it as you move through your analysis and see an unexpected feature of talk or text that is worthy of attention. For example, in a project on off-label use of antidepressants (i.e., the use of antidepressants with diagnosable conditions for which they were not designed, tested, or approved by a regulatory body), my initial interest was in how people who have received a diagnosis for something other than anxiety or depression (e.g., insomnia, restless leg syndrome, new daily persistent headaches) talk about having been given a prescription for an antidepressant. In my first pass through the data, I unexpectedly became interested in how these interviewees oriented to the topic of depression, despite no interview questions being explicitly directed to it. I then decided to focus on this feature of the interview data for my first analysis in this project (see McMullen, 2016).

It is also possible that you might come across an unanticipated source of data that can inform your general question and decide to focus on this source, either alone or in conjunction with your planned source. For example, after coediting a book on women and depression in social context with

Janet Stoppard (Stoppard & McMullen, 2003), I happened on two fact sheets on depression on the website of the Canadian Psychological Association. After reading these two fact sheets, I was struck by how differently the conjunction of women and depression was (and was not) presented in them, compared with how the authors in our book had presented it (see McMullen, 2008; McMullen & Stoppard, 2006). In this case, my general topic (women and depression) and my broad research question (How is the conjunction of women and depression constructed?) remained the same, but the specific questions I asked were formulated with the context in mind. For my chapter in our book, I relied on conversations from psychotherapy sessions and asked, "How [is] the gendered, devalued condition we now call 'depression' . . . constituted in the lives of women who have been diagnosed as 'depressed'?" (McMullen, 2003, p. 18). For my analyses of the fact sheets, I formulated my research question in slightly different ways, depending on the publication outlet. For an article published in a special issue on feminism in Canadian psychology, we focused on "the extent to which a gendered understanding of depression has informed Canadian psychology's public discourse on depression" (McMullen & Stoppard, 2006, p. 273). For a chapter in a book on narratives of depression, I framed the issue as "How these 'official' psychological narratives [i.e., the fact sheets] reference the gendered nature of depression" (p. 128) and undertook a narrative rather than a discursive analysis of the data (McMullen, 2008). So, you should expect, at least on occasion, to engage in iterative cycling between the statement of your topic and the articulation of your research question(s) according to your developing analysis, the availability of data sources, and the focus of your publication outlet.

DETERMINING WHAT TYPE OF DATA TO COLLECT OR GENERATE TO ADDRESS YOUR RESEARCH QUESTIONS

Because talk and text are ubiquitous in human life, the possible sources of data for discursive research are virtually limitless. Data can be textual (e.g., from books, newspaper, or magazine articles; transcriptions of debates; pamphlets; diary entries); in the form of talk (e.g., from archival recordings of speeches, conversations, and interviews or from interviews or focus groups conducted solely for the purpose of your research; telephone helplines); from online sources (e.g., websites, chat rooms and forums, comments sections, emails, tweets); and combined with other sensory data, such as the visual (e.g., movies, posters) and/or auditory (e.g., songs). The important aspect in deciding what type of data to collect or generate is the fit of the data source to your research question.

In the title of this section, I have deliberately used the words "collect" and "generate." I do so to draw out an important distinction between data that exist independently of your research project—for example, archival or ongoing production of material that would exist in the absence of your project—and data that are produced for your particular project—material that would not otherwise exist were it not for your research project. Data of the former type might be thought of as being "collected" or "gathered" and those of the latter type as being "generated." Most often, data of the latter type are produced in the form of the research interview, typically in which you (the researcher) serve as the interviewer of persons who can inform your topic (i.e., the interviewees). The word "generate" draws attention not only to the notion that, in the case of research interviews, the data are "got up" for the purposes of the project but also that you (or others) as the interviewer are intricately a part of the data that are produced.

I will have more to say about the affordances and pitfalls of various methods of data collection or generation for discursive research in the next chapter. However, at this point, the important message is that when designing your study, think creatively and carefully about which source(s) of data might inform your research question(s), and do not automatically resort to the research interview as the method of choice, despite its popularity in qualitative research generally. In addition, continue to reflect on how your choice of method of data collection or generation influences the data that will be available to you for analysis and how these data will influence what you have to say in relation to your research question. In other words, remember that every choice you make with regard to the design of your project shapes the context of your study.

Deciding to Use Archival Documents

If you determine that an already existing source (or already existing sources) of talk and text is available and suitable for addressing your research question(s), you will most likely then have to specify how you will choose items from these sources for subsequent analysis. On occasion, a single item (e.g., a book, movie, debate, television interview) might be determined to be a particularly rich source of data to address your question(s). Such was the case, for example, when Abell and Stokoe (2001) chose the *Panorama* interview between Martin Bashir and Princess Diana as the data for a question on how culturally situated identities are located in this particular context. In this instance, you would justify your selection decision on the basis of the exemplary nature of the particular item for your research question.

Most often, however, you will likely have to select a limited number of items from your data source for analysis. In this instance, you will have to develop a set of selection criteria and provide a justification for these criteria. For example, one of my former students, Agitha Valiakalayil, was interested in how the text of self-help websites is used to construct the relation between stress and depression. In fashioning her selection criteria, she had to consider questions such as "Which search engines will I use to access relevant websites?" "Which search terms will I use?" and "How will I decide which specific websites to select?" Her answers to these questions contained both her selection criteria and her justification for these criteria:

> I began data collection by entering relevant terms using the Google search engine, as this is primarily the way that website users access online information on a particular topic. In particular, I entered terms such as "stress," "depression," and "self-help." I reviewed the search results and focused on sites where the stated goal was to provide assistance with the self-management of symptoms of stress and depression. . . . I focused my analysis on the top ten ranked websites as individuals online are found to rarely search beyond the first page of results. (Valiakalayil, 2015, pp. 43–44).

This example illustrates the question you should ask yourself when you have determined that archival data will enable you to address your research question(s): Of all possible existing sources (online and offline) of data, which items will I select, how, and why? Keeping a record or journal of these selection decisions will be useful when preparing the presentations and writing the manuscript(s) that follow from your analyses. In addition, this record will help you remain focused on the need to keep asking yourself, "What might be the effect of my data-selection decisions on what I produce from my analysis?" In other words, "How do my decisions shape the context (and outcome) of my study?"

Deciding to Select and Recruit Research Participants to Projects in Which Data Are Generated

If you determine that your research question necessitates that you generate new data to address it, you might decide to use research interviews or focus groups as a method for engaging in talk related to your topic. This choice requires that you develop criteria for selecting participants. These criteria typically specify requirements for being included or excluded from your study (e.g., age, gender or sexual identity, ethnicity, occupation, knowledge of or familiarity with your topic). For example, in a project on off-label prescribing and use of antidepressants (McMullen, 2016), I set my inclusion criteria as (a) being of legal age to consent to participate (18 years and older), (b) having received a prescription for an antidepressant, and (c) having received this prescription for a diagnosis other than depression or anxiety. These criteria enabled me to screen out adults who had received a prescription for medication other than an antidepressant or who had received a prescription for an antidepressant in response to a diagnosis of depression or its often comorbid condition of anxiety.

After determining who can inform your research question(s) and what format you will use for generating your data (e.g., one-on-one interviews, focus groups), you will have to decide how to recruit participants to your study. In my projects and those of most of my students, we typically use posters, online spaces, or personalized letters of invitation. Deciding where to place posters depends on whom you want to attract to your project and how relatively heterogeneous or homogeneous you want your sample to be. In recruiting female participants for a focus group project on how women engaged with direct-to-consumer advertisements for antidepressants, another student of mine, Christine Babineau, decided to place paper posters on bulletin boards at our local university, on outdoor bulletin boards throughout the downtown core of our city, and in some local businesses. She also uploaded electronic versions to our university's online announcements and to the community events section of Kijiji.ca, an online classified service for posting local advertisements (Babineau et al., 2017). For this project, because the only inclusion criterion was that participants be women of legal age who were interested in participating, we wanted to maximize the heterogeneity of our sample by advertising broadly. In a project on family physicians' accounts of their diagnostic and treatment practices for depression (McMullen, 2012), I decided to send personalized letters of invitation to participate in the study to all family physicians who were listed in our city's telephone directory. In this case, I targeted my recruitment efforts to a specific group and reasoned that a personalized invitation might be more appealing and persuasive than a notice of the study posted on an office bulletin board. Regardless of the method of recruitment, it is important to keep a record of who responded to your recruitment material (e.g., relevant demographic and project-related details), who was selected for participation, who was excluded from participating, and why.

Again, in deciding whom, how, and where to recruit, you are setting the context(s) for your study and, thereby, influencing the data that will be available to you for analysis. Sometimes, it is as important to try to determine or speculate about who was not included through your recruitment efforts as it is to specify who was included. In other words, how did your recruitment efforts advantage the participation of some persons and disadvantage that of others? Reflecting on the outcome of your recruitment efforts can lead, on occasion, to future projects that are designed to include those who were either eliminated or otherwise excluded from your present project.

3 COLLECTING AND GENERATING DATA

After you have decided which sources of data you are going to draw on to address your research question, the task of actually collecting and/or generating the data typically forms the next stage of your research project. However, before you undertake this task, you will have to determine whether an application for ethics approval from your or other institutions is required. When using archival data in the public domain, it is often the case that such an application is not necessary. Even in this case, it is still a good idea to check with your institutional ethics body (and/or key members of other institutions who might have a stake in your project) for exceptions that require approval. However, if you are going to be generating new data through, for example, interviews or focus groups, you will almost certainly have to submit an application and wait until it is approved before beginning the process of generating data. Be sure to check with your institution and adhere to local protocols to secure the necessary approvals.

https://doi.org/10.1037/0000220-003
Essentials of Discursive Psychology, by L. M. McMullen

COLLECTING ARCHIVAL OR ALREADY EXISTING DATA

If you have decided that analyzing one archived unit (e.g., an episode of a television show, a particular debate) or an exemplary unit of already existing data (e.g., a book, a song, a limited collection of posters) will best enable you to address your research question(s), collecting the data should be relatively straightforward. On occasion, multiple versions of what appears to be the same unit (e.g., a book, an advertisement on YouTube) might exist, so be sure to record which version you select for analysis. Remember that links to online material can be broken, so try to preserve a hard, photographed, or electronic copy of the unit, if possible, without violating any applicable copyright legislation.

If multiple units of such data exist, you will have to decide which units to select. While keeping your focus on selecting material that addresses your research question(s), you should also be attentive to the importance of ensuring variability in your data. Discursive analysis often benefits from showing different patterns of language use, and sometimes this variability is achieved through deliberately choosing disparate units for analysis. Such was the case in my and Janet Stoppard's analysis of how the conjunction of women and depression was constructed in online fact sheets designed for public consumption (McMullen & Stoppard, 2006). In addition to choosing for analysis two fact sheets on depression (one on depression and one on postpartum depression) that were available on the website of the Canadian Psychological Association (CPA), we searched the Web for other material that could serve as a contrast. We chose a fact sheet on women and mental health produced by the World Health Organization (WHO) that, in contrast to the psychologically oriented fact sheets on the CPA website, focused on situating depression in the context of women's lives. The WHO fact sheet essentially functioned as a foil for our analysis of the CPA documents and, in doing so, sharpened our analyses of these documents.

The availability of data from online sources (e.g., blogs, chat forums, comments on articles in the media, social media sites) has come with both opportunities and challenges for discursive researchers. Although ensuring endless amounts of potential data, questions regarding what to select and how to determine when to stop selecting items for analysis can be rather daunting. What is important is that you document the details of which sites you sample from and when, your criteria for including and excluding items from your sample, and your rationale for these criteria. All these decisions will shape the context of your study and should be borne in mind as you embark on the analyses of your data and the eventual writing of presentations and manuscripts based on these analyses. If possible, storing the data in their original form (e.g., via screenshots) is preferred because doing so will allow you to preserve text and graphics.

Determining when you have sufficient data for analysis is often not an easy decision. Sometimes the decision is pragmatic (e.g., when a project is driven by a date for completion). Most often, however, the decision is based on the sense that you have enough data to address your research question(s). Because data collection and preliminary moves into analysis (e.g., initial readings, making note of some of the obvious actions being performed in the talk or text) often go hand in hand in discursive projects, you will likely develop a sense of the quality of your corpus of data (and the potential quality of the analysis you can produce) while you are compiling it. Although there are no established criteria for determining when you have collected sufficient data, dwelling in the data during the process of collecting them (e.g., scanning parts, perhaps focusing more intently on others) should enable you to determine that the data are relevant to your topic and sense whether there are some broad patterns and variations in patterns in the data that can be worked up to address your research question(s). Of course, you can always decide well into the process of analysis that you have to collect more data. But, typically, the decision to stop collecting data is based on your sense that you have a rich enough set of data to produce an analysis of good quality.

GENERATING DATA FROM INTERVIEWS OR FOCUS GROUPS

The research interview and, to a lesser extent, the focus group are frequently used ways of generating data for qualitative investigations. Despite the ubiquity of these methods, the research interview, in particular, is not without its critics (e.g., Potter & Hepburn, 2005; Silverman, 2017). The main thrust of the criticisms is that, although the interview is often conceptualized as a way of getting at something that is authentically human, it is actually a contrived and (explicitly and implicitly) regulated human interaction. For example, each participant in the interview likely has a prescribed role in the interaction, along with a particular stake or interest in the project. There is typically an interviewer (who is also frequently the researcher undertaking the project for a particular reason, such as for a thesis or an external stakeholder) and an interviewee (who is specifically recruited and agrees to participate because of having knowledge of the topic being investigated). The format is likely to be that of question or comment from the interviewer, followed by a response from the interviewee. The point to remember is that these features influence the data you will generate from the research interview and what you will produce from your project, just as other sources of data (e.g., blogs, radio programs, chat rooms, speeches) are shaped by their contexts.

Despite these concerns, interviews and focus groups remain oft-used ways of generating data for discursive projects. If you decide to use interviews, you should ask yourself what kind of interview you want to conduct and what kind of relationship you want to establish with your interviewees. Do you want to use a relational, empathic approach (e.g., Josselson, 2013)? Do you want to join with your interviewee in adopting a critical stance on your topic (e.g., Parker, 2005)? Or do you want to position yourself as the interested outsider? You should try to think through the possible consequences of the stance you choose and its implications for the kind of data that will be generated. Of course, any preplanned stance will be molded by the dynamics of the interview (e.g., by how much or how little the interviewee talks, by your unexpected reactions to how the interviewee responds to your questions and comments, by how you and the interviewee work to position each other). What is important to recognize, however, is that, in the role of the interviewer, you are never a neutral question-asker.

Although having experience in conducting interviews is not a prerequisite for using them in a research project, it is a good idea to read a few different sources on the topic of interviewing and interview-based qualitative research (e.g., Josselson, 2013; Magnusson & Marecek, 2015) before beginning to generate your data. These sources provide suggestions and advice on aspects such as planning the interview, designing the interview guide, doing the interview, the importance of listening, and features of good, poor, and difficult interviews.

In constructing your interview protocol, it is often best to strive for fewer, rather than more, questions or comments on your topic. These questions or comments should be quite open ended and allow interviewees considerable latitude in their responses. For example, in a study I conducted on discourses of patient–physician decision making in family physicians' accounts of their diagnostic and treatment practices for depression (McMullen, 2012), I used the following sorts of comments, questions, and probes in my interviews with these physicians:

- Describe the nature of your family practice.

- Describe how you go about determining whether one of your patients is depressed.

- Do you use a screening device?
- Do you rely on *Diagnostic and Statistical Manual of Mental Disorders, Fifth Edition* (*DSM-5*; American Psychiatric Association, 2013) criteria?
- Do you use a list of necessary and sufficient criteria?

• Describe how you determine whether, and how, to treat a patient for depression.

• For what reasons, or under what circumstances, do you prescribe antidepressants?

• Do you recommend treatments other than antidepressants for depression? If so, what do you recommend, and under what circumstances?

• Do you experience any dilemmas in your diagnostic and treatment practices for depression (e.g., believing that antidepressants are the treatment of choice for a particular patient but wanting to support that patient's decision not to take antidepressants)?

Rather than being a rigid format, such comments, questions, and probes should serve as a guide to covering the topic of your study and as a way to open up a conversation between you and the interviewee.

A frequently asked question with regard to using interviews to generate data is "How many are enough?" There is no simple answer to this question (see Baker & Edwards, 2012). Because discursive research typically involves detailed analyses of a limited number of extracts of data relevant to your research question, it is not unusual for a data set to comprise relatively few interviews. For example, projects I have worked on have included as few as six (McMullen & Herman, 2009) and as many as 13 interviews (McMullen, 2016). Again, what is most important is that you have a corpus of data that is sufficient enough to permit you to identify patterns (and variations in patterns) that are relevant to your research question(s).

Conducting focus groups is another method of generating data for discursive studies. However, unlike the use of this method as a means for eliciting opinions, beliefs, or preferences of participants (as is often how they are understood by researchers who use other qualitative methodologies), focus groups in discursive research are treated as sites of interaction and are studied for what they can yield in and of themselves (Puchta & Potter, 2004). Because the format of such groups typically involves a moderator (again, often the researcher) and a group of people who are brought together to talk about a particular topic, this method should be used when you are interested in studying how people negotiate a conversation about a topic.

In these groups, participants typically take positions on a topic, formulate arguments and counterarguments, and agree and disagree with each other. It is important to remember, then, that the data generated from this method are a coconstruction not just between the moderator and each participant but among the participants themselves. Focus groups are not interviews and should not be treated as such.

As is the case with all discursive studies, the choice of this method should align with your research question(s). For example, Christine Babineau chose focus groups rather than individual interviews for her study on women's meaning making in the context of viewing direct-to-consumer television advertisements for antidepressants because she was interested in how women negotiate the multiple meanings of what constitutes depression (Babineau et al., 2017). As with the decision to use interviews, you should acquaint yourself with available resources on conceptualizing, designing, and conducting studies using focus groups (e.g., Barbour, 2018).

Recording and Transcribing

Because discursive analyses require careful attention to what is said and how it is said, you must ensure that you acquire high-quality audio (or audio–video) recordings of interviews and focus groups. After securing the recordings, you will most likely want to transcribe them in their entirety, being sure not to omit features such as uhs, mhms, and yeahs; repetitions of words; sighs; laughter; and crying that are part of a stream of talk. I highly recommend that you do your own transcribing because careful listening to the recordings during transcribing will familiarize you with your data and will continue the early phases of data analysis, which will have already begun if you conducted the interviews or focus groups yourself.

Notational Detail

Deciding on the level of notational detail to insert in your transcripts is not a trivial matter. The system of notations typically recommended by discursive psychologists who focus primarily on the micro features of talk and how something is said is the comprehensive set of symbols associated with Jefferson (2004). Although using the full Jefferson (2004) system in all your transcripts might be considered ideal, it is time consuming and often found by readers to be distracting, particularly if you are not referring to these notations consistently in your analysis. If your research question does not require the kind of precise focus that is necessary in conversation analytic work, it is possible to compromise and use what has been deemed "Jefferson lite" (although see criticisms of this approach, e.g., Potter & Hepburn, 2005; see Appendix B for a partial list of frequently used notations). It is also possible to use either the full Jefferson system or Jefferson lite on only those extracts chosen for analysis, rather than to populate the entire transcript with the notations. The point here is that you will have to decide whether including the full Jefferson notation in the extracts you choose for analysis is potentially more informative for your reader (i.e., it might permit them to "hear" the extract) or more distracting (i.e., if you do not attend to many of these features in your analysis). Regardless of the level of notational detail you choose to use in your transcripts, be sure to insert line numbers (usually at the left side of every line of text) so that you can easily find segments of text during your analysis. Extracts that are subjected to detailed analysis and used in publications and presentations should retain numbered lines because you will have to refer to specific lines when warranting your analytic claims.

4

ANALYZING YOUR DATA

As I noted in Chapter 1, my focus in this book is on how you can use the principles of discursive psychology, including critical discursive psychology, to address both how people use features of language in talk and text and with what effects and which resources they draw on when speaking and writing. In this chapter, I outline suggestions for how to go about analyzing your data from these perspectives and provide illustrations from some of my work.

A PROCESS OF DATA ANALYSIS

Before presenting a process of data analysis, a caveat is in order: Engaging in data analysis in discursive psychology is not a lockstep process. Although I present a set of activities in a particular order, expect to cycle back through them, perhaps in various orders, while conducting your analysis.

Readings and Listenings

After having collected or generated and transcribed your data, it is important to refamiliarize yourself with your entire corpus of data. I recommend first

https://doi.org/10.1037/0000220-004
Essentials of Discursive Psychology, by L. M. McMullen

reading and/or listening to the entire data set as a whole in an undirected way, without making notes or focusing in on any aspect in particular. If you have both recordings and transcripts or other textual material available to you, move between these different mediums so you can take advantage of what each has to offer. Allow the data to wash over you so that you get a feel for the corpus as a whole.

Making Notes

In subsequent readings and listenings, start to engage with your data in more directed ways. I prefer to work from hard copies of my data, but you can certainly work from electronic copies. It is also possible to use software packages, such as, as of this writing, ATLAS.ti, MAXQDA, and NVivo, for inserting notes and comments in your data. Although these packages cannot tell you what to note or comment on, they can be useful in organizing your data and retrieving specific extracts of data for more intensive analysis. While working with transcripts or other texts, I make lots of notes in the margins and circle or underline passages that strike me. At this stage, while I have my topic and my tentative research question(s) in mind, I opt for being inclusive in what I attend to and try not to foreclose on possibly interesting foci for later, in-depth analysis.

Four sensitizing strategies outlined by Wood and Kroger (2000, pp. 91–95) can be helpful at this early stage. One, begin by starting to identify what is going on in your data. It can often be helpful to be aware of your first reactions to the data and to note in the text what these reactions are and where they occur. Noting where they occur can assist you in trying to articulate what in your data is contributing to these reactions. For example, your first reaction to hearing interviewees talk about using antidepressants might be that they are defending their decision to do so. You then note that your reaction is tied, in part, to the interviewees' use of words such as "real" or "true" to present their depression in contrast to that of others, which is characterized by phrases such as "not clinical depression." Second, do not ignore the obvious. For example, speakers and writers often make use of anecdotes or short stories in their accounts of events. Rather than taking narratives for granted, you might note when such anecdotes and stories appear in your data. Third, focus more on what the speaker or writer is doing, rather than on the content or meaning of the talk or text. That is, try to note and label what actions are being performed by speakers and writers (e.g., apologizing, blaming, praising, deflecting). Four, take note of what is not present in your data. For example, you might note that writers of media articles on depression focus primarily on girls and women and make no mention of adolescent boys.

Noting what is said or written and how it is said or written requires that you familiarize yourself with the terminology for, and exemplars of, the many discursive devices and resources that have been identified in the language in which you are working. This process is an ongoing one (even for seasoned researchers), as new devices and resources come into use by speakers and writers, which are subsequently identified, analyzed, and foregrounded in the literature. In addition, it is a process that can be engaged in at any stage of your research. However, making notes and inserting comments in your data is a good time for continuing with this process of familiarization because doing so will sensitize you to the presence of these devices and resources in your data. For comprehensive lists of the most common devices in the English language that are relied on by discursive psychologists, see Wiggins (2017) and Wood and Kroger (2000). In Appendix C, I provide a sample of some of the most common devices and resources with which you should be familiar.

Selecting Extracts of Data That Speak to Your Research Question(s)

Following these initial ventures into your data, you will likely determine whether you adhere to your original research question(s), slightly alter it (or them), or focus on another question that is driven by the data themselves. The next step will be to solidify your research question(s) and then to select extracts or parts of your corpus of data that you judge as speaking to your question(s). I recommend having a clear research question in mind (e.g., How do commenters on online articles about antidepressants defend against critiques of the use of antidepressants?) before intensively analyzing your data. Otherwise, you can run the risk of feeling overwhelmed by your data and not knowing where to begin.

In this early stage of selecting extracts or parts of data, I opt for being overly inclusive rather than tightly exclusive. If a portion of data appears to have some relevance to my research question(s), I will include it. For example, after conducting a set of interviews with persons who had been prescribed an antidepressant for a diagnosis other than depression or anxiety (often referred to as off-label), I became interested in how the interviewees used the category of depression in their accounts of this event (McMullen, 2016). I then extracted every segment of the interviews in which talk of depression occurred. As you identify extracts that speak to your research question(s), create a separate file of these extracts.

Readings and Grouping of Extracts

Once you have created this separate file, I recommend engaging in the same process as you did when working with the full corpus of data. First, read and reread this smaller data set in an undirected way to familiarize yourself with this more focused domain. Then, engage in more directed readings that enable you to sharpen your focus on what is going on in this subset of data. If desired, you can group your extracts into broad clusters. For example, if your research question focuses on how a particular practice, event, or category of persons is constructed, you might group together those extracts that seem to have something in common. For instance, if you were doing a study on how parenting is constructed by young adults, you might have separate clusters of extracts that speak to "parenting as watching and protecting," "parenting as laissez-faire," and "parenting as democracy." Although extracts grouped into a cluster will likely have some commonalities among them, they will also likely vary in interesting ways that can be focused on in your analyses. For example, you might notice that extracts grouped into the "parenting as watching and protecting" cluster display a variety of social actions being performed by speakers or writers, such as denying, affirming, criticizing, or being sarcastic. Or you might notice that a speaker or writer takes up more than one of these constructions in a short extract. In this case, you might include the extract in more than one cluster. To be clear, these clusters (and the boundaries between them) are not meant to be mutually exclusive and rigid; rather, they are simply a way of beginning to organize your data according to broad patterns.

I usually assign a name to each of these clusters, again as a way of beginning to articulate broad patterns. For example, in my work on how persons talked about depression in their accounts of having received a prescription for an antidepressant for a condition other than depression or anxiety, I named my clusters (a) denying being depressed; (b) separating one's symptoms from those that define depression; (c) normalizing mild, situationally based depression as secondary to one's primary diagnosis; (d) equating low doses of an antidepressant with the medication not being used as an antidepressant; and (e) constructing others as providing implicit and explicit reassurance that the antidepressant was not being prescribed for depression. Labeling the clusters in this way enabled me not only to articulate some broad patterns in the data but also to keep a focus on (some of) what the interviewees were doing with their talk.

Deciding Which Extracts to Analyze and Write Up in Detail

As I have mentioned previously, in addressing your research question(s), you will select extracts of talk or text from your full corpus of data. However, the number of extracts you deem relevant to your research question(s) is usually considerably larger than the number you select for intensive analysis and write up. Although having a clearly articulated, standardized set of criteria for selecting this smaller subset of extracts might be considered desirable (even comforting), I often think in broad, rather loosely articulated criteria. I typically select a few extracts that I deem to be quite clear exemplars of each part of the argument (i.e., the analytic points) I am making (e.g., about how a category, practice, event, etc., is being constructed or about what social actions are being performed), along with another few extracts that nuance, complicate, or even contradict the supposedly clear exemplars but which enable me to enrich my argument. Remember that you should focus on variations in how speakers or writers use specific linguistic devices and/or resources and to what ends, so selecting a subset of extracts for intensive analysis that is representative of the domain of extracts that speak to your research question(s) is important.

I often find that there is a dynamic and iterative interplay between formulating my argument, selecting the set of extracts for intensive analysis, and analyzing these extracts. I might begin by noticing something of interest in my data that is relevant to my research question(s) and developing a loose argument. As I select a set of extracts for intensive analysis and undertake the analysis of them, my argument can sometimes begin to take a slightly different form than was originally (loosely) formulated. This more fully articulated argument can then shape subsequent readings of the extracts I have already analyzed, which, in turn, can result in modifications of my written analyses. On occasion, this process can result in the substitution of a previously unselected (and subsequently analyzed) extract for an already analyzed extract. My point here is that you will likely cycle through the process of selecting a subset of extracts for detailed analysis as you engage in this analysis.

But what does analysis look like when you use this methodology? For most of the remainder of this chapter, I take you through examples of detailed analyses of extracts from three research studies I and my students have conducted. In doing so, I illustrate how you make analytic claims from your data and how you provide evidence for (or warrant) these claims. In reading these examples, you might look for how I have tried to avoid the pitfalls of underanalysis proposed by Antaki et al. (2003). According to these authors, common forms of underanalysis in discursive studies include

- summarizing what is being said by speakers or writers, often in the form of themes;

- listing a string of quotations or an isolated quotation as evidence for your analytic claim(s) without linking these claims to features in the quoted material;

- spotting and naming features in the quoted extracts without making claims about the functions that are being performed through the speaker's or writer's use of such features; and

- claiming to have discovered the use of particular discourses in your data by providing evidentiary examples from the talk or text without explaining the basis for the claim that such discourses exist outside the context of your data.

As Antaki et al. stated, "Discourse analysis means doing analysis" (p. 1).

EXAMPLES OF DETAILED ANALYSES OF EXTRACTS OF DATA

Example 1: How a Particular Discursive Device Is Deployed and With What Effects

Discursive analysts are sometimes interested in how particular linguistic or rhetorical devices, such as those listed in Appendix C, are used in talk or text. Here, I illustrate how Kristjan Sigurdson and I went about analyzing constituents of the "depression is to diabetes as antidepressants are to insulin" analogy that occurred without prompting in interviews with family physicians who treat depression and with long-term users of antidepressants. This illustration is an example of how data that are originally generated for one purpose—in this case, to investigate either how family physicians construct the decision-making process with regard to diagnosing depression and prescribing antidepressants or other treatments (McMullen, 2012) or how long-term users of antidepressants talk about such usage in the face of public controversy about antidepressants (Sigurdson & McMullen, 2013)—can be used to address an unplanned and unanticipated research question.

First, let me summarize the process we followed before showing how we analyzed a couple of extracts. After becoming intrigued that our interviewees used constituents of this analogy (i.e., "depression is to diabetes" or "antidepressants are to insulin") without being explicitly prompted to do so, we first extracted all instances of the use of these constituents from the interviews and put them into a separate file. We then iteratively engaged in the following activities: (a) reading and rereading the segments of text containing the constituents in the context in which they occurred in the interviews; (b) familiarizing ourselves with what constitutes diabetes (both Type 1 and Type 2), how the different types manifest, are diagnosed and treated or managed, and are understood clinically and societally; (c) familiarizing ourselves with the structure of an analogy and how this figure of speech is thought to function; and (d) focusing in on our extracted instances of the constituents of the analogy to articulate how we came to see the analogy as unraveling or not holding up. We then loosely articulated these ways as (a) the constituents of the analogy or inferences (e.g., about the discernible presence of a biomarker, about the certainty of diagnosis) that can be derived from constituents of the analogy do not correspond; (b) the constituents of the analogy do not correspond even in the case of type II diabetes; and (c) use of the analogy does not have the desired effects. These practices assisted us in remaining grounded in the context from which our data were derived, educating ourselves about the substance and form of the "depression is to diabetes as antidepressants are to insulin" analogy, and attuning ourselves to seeing variation in our data.

Now, let us consider the following extract from an interview with a family physician who provides care for patients who are diagnosed as depressed. In the extract, "I" denotes "interviewer" and "P" denotes "physician." This extract follows immediately from talk about the difficulty of accessing psychiatric services for persons who are diagnosed as depressed. We saw this extract as illustrating how the constituents or inferences of the analogy do not correspond.

In our analysis of this extract, we focused primarily on how the phrase "would be nice to have a little blood test" in line 2 disrupts the "depression is to diabetes" constituent of the analogy. Let me unpack how I work through this extract to come to this claim. To establish that the interviewee is invoking this constituent, I take the interviewee's phrase "what are the deficiencies (.) which of these neurotransmitters (1) [are at fault]" in line 2 as referencing the widely held understanding of depression as caused by an imbalance of neurochemicals in the brain. So, here, we can see that the interviewee orients to the focus in my question in line 1, on "people who are (.) depressed," with an implicit reference to depression as a biologically based medical condition. This implicit reference is immediately followed in

EXTRACT 1

1. I: is there anything else that you feel hinders your care (.) of (.) people who are (.) depressed

2. PO2: (1) would be nice to have a little blood test that would show (.) which are- what are the deficiencies (.) which of these neurotransmitters (1) [are at fault]

3. I: [wouldn't it]((*chuckling*)) (.) [exactly]

4. PO2: [(.) like is] it thyroid or diabetes ((*chuckling*)) [(.) right]

5. I: [yeah exactly] (.) exactly (.) just the [uncertainty of really-]

6. PO2: [yeah (.) you know] (.) put a thumbprint on this thing and (1) the arrow shows you (.) which ones to choose

7. I: Yeah exactly (.h)-

8. PO2: It'll come

line 4 by the phrase "[(.) like is] it thyroid or diabetes," which, through the use of "like," sets up a comparison of depression with "thyroid or diabetes" and implicates the "depression is to diabetes" constituent of the analogy.

With the presence of this constituent of the analogy established in this extract, I focus primarily on how the interviewee's phrase "would be nice to have a little <u>b</u>lood test" disrupts this constituent, specifically with respect to the certainty regarding a differential diagnosis. Specifically, I note the interviewee's use of modal verbs "would" ("would be nice to have" [line 2]) and "will" ("it'll come" [line 8]). In this context, these verbs implicate the degree to which he presents himself as having the ability to perform a particular activity (see Wiggins, 2017, p. 173)—in this case, making a differential diagnosis. Because these verbs reference a desired future possibility or probability, I argue that the interviewee is making a claim that, unlike "thyroid or diabetes," which can be differentially diagnosed with certainty via a blood test, no such test presently exists for depression, and without such a test, it is difficult for him to diagnose depression definitively. So, I conclude that the "depression is to diabetes" constituent of the analogy falters in this extract because the assumed comparability between depression and diabetes does not hold with respect to the possibility of achieving diagnostic accuracy.

A few features of this presentation of my analysis are worth noting. First, I explicitly connected parts of talk with my analytic claims. As is always required in discursive research of this kind, you have to show your audience which part(s) of the talk or text forms the basis of your claims. Using numbered lines and including specific segments of talk or text in your detailed analysis accomplishes this requirement. Second, I made explicit how I was reasoning from what I deemed as implicit in the data. Such moves are a necessary way of being transparent and showing your audience how you are coming to your claims. Third, I returned to the question of "if so, then what?" throughout my analysis. Returning to this focus is a good way of reminding yourself that drawing out the possible implications and consequences of particular discursive practices is an important part of the analysis. Fourth, because the purpose of the study from which this extract is drawn was to focus on how speakers took up the analogy and to justify my claim that how they did so provided evidence of the unraveling of the analogy, I focused on the constituents of the analogy itself and ignored other features of the extract. For example, although I inserted notational details into our transcribed extracts, I did not refer to these details in my analysis. Specifically, I did not interpret the chuckling or the overlapping speech that occurs on the part of both speakers. Nor did I focus more broadly on the interactional exchange between myself and the interviewee. The point here is that to not get overwhelmed by the number of possible analytic foci in your data, you will have to stay focused on your research question and the level of analysis that addresses it.

Consider another extract from the same data set—this one from an interview with a long-term user of antidepressants and also considered by us to illustrate how the constituents of the analogy do not correspond. We chose this extract for analysis for two reasons: (a) because it was from an interview with a long-term user of antidepressants, and we wanted to show how the "depression is to diabetes as antidepressants are to insulin" analogy was disrupted in the talk of both patients and physicians and (b) because we wanted to include extracts from each part of the analogy (i.e., the con-structed link between depression and diabetes and between antidepressants and insulin) to illustrate the potential scope of the disruption. This segment of talk follows from the interviewee's claim that her doctors tell her that her depression is a "life-long thing" and that she should stay on antidepressants, to which she counters that she wishes to be "medication-free" and that she and her friends who are also on antidepressants "ALL feel bad" that they are on them.

As with Extract 1, in working up this segment of talk, I want to establish that the focus of my analysis—the "depression is to diabetes as antidepres-sants are to insulin" analogy—is present. I note that the "antidepressants are to insulin" constituent of this analogy appears as a simile in lines 3 to 4 but

EXTRACT 2

1. LTO5: there's always this (1) this idea of what am I like without them (1) 'cause is it (.)
2. is it <u>changing</u> my <u>personality</u> (.) or <u>who I am</u> (.) do you know what I mean 'cause like- (.)
3. an- and then you have people who say oh well it's (.) it's kind of like (.) um (2) if you
4. have diabetes you have to take insulin and stuff and I say <u>yeah</u> but those medications (.)
5. aren't (.) messing (.) with your <u>neurons</u> ((laughs)) you know what I mean like they
6. aren't (.) um (.) like it <u>doesn't</u> <u>really</u> change your (.) your <u>mind</u> whereas I wonder
7. sometimes if this changes my mind (.) what I would be like without them

also that it is preceded by the qualifier "kind of," which can set up the comparison of antidepressants with insulin as not entirely apt. I also note that the interviewee uses reported speech—features of speech that attribute the source of talk to another speaker (see Wiggins, 2017, p. 166)—to invoke this constituent of the analogy. Specifically, the interviewee uses the phrase "people who say" (line 3), which in this case, appears to serve as a way for the interviewee to distance herself from what she is claiming others are saying about the aptness of insulin to antidepressants. That is, the interviewee is only reporting others' use of this constituent of the analogy, not using it herself.

In focusing on the structure of Extract 2, I see that it is set up as an argument, with an opening position presented by the interviewee (lines 1–2), followed by two rebuttals in the form of reported speech—the first attributed to other "people" (lines 3–4) and the second voiced by the interviewee (lines 4–6)—and a return to the opening position in line 7 ("What I would be like without them"). Using the "antidepressants are to insulin" constituent of the analogy as the nub of this argument, the interviewee can differentiate the effects of using antidepressants from the effects of using insulin and develop the position she asserts in lines 1 to 2. I turn to the substance of what the interviewee claims does not work in this analogy to determine how she constructs the difference between insulin and antidepressants (lines 4–6)—specifically, that, in contrast to antidepressants, medications for diabetes "aren't (.) messing (.) with your <u>neurons</u> ((laughs)) you know what I mean like they aren't (.) um (.) like it <u>doesn't</u> <u>really</u> change your (.) your <u>mind</u>" (lines 5–6). Her emphasis on words such as "neurons" and "mind," which is signaled by the underlining, alerts me to the possible importance and significance of these words and phrases in her argument. That is, according to the interviewee's argument, there is something about the effects of antidepressants on the brain and mind that renders the analogy to the effects of insulin on the cells of the pancreas as not apt. In light of what the interviewee says in line 2—"is it <u>changing</u> my <u>personality</u> (.) or <u>who I am</u>"—I interpret the interviewee as making an argument that there is something qualitatively different between the effects of antidepressants and the effects of insulin, with the former affecting one's neurons and possibly one's mind, personality, and personhood, and the latter not (although note that the interviewee is silent on how she constructs the effects of insulin). I conclude, then, that this difference challenges the aptness of this constituent of the analogy.

A few additional points about what you can keep in mind while doing a discursive analysis can be drawn from how I worked with Extract 2. First, do not immediately ignore or dismiss what might seem inconsequential (e.g., use of phrases such as "kind of" or emphases placed on certain words). Sometimes, paying attention to these discursive devices can assist you in developing a robust analysis. Second, think in terms of the possible function(s) that might be served by the use of particular discursive devices and be prepared to interpret these functions (e.g., how I saw the speaker in this extract as distancing herself from the "antidepressants are to insulin" constituent by using reported speech attributed to others and then rebutting this speech). Third, remember that you are making an argument via your analysis and that you have to keep returning your focus to this argument as you work with your data. In working with Extract 2, I had to remind myself that my focus was on showing how the interviewee's talk supported my argument about the unraveling of the "depression is to diabetes as antidepressants are to insulin" analogy.

The following is a general comment on discursive analyses of how a particular discursive device is deployed and with what effects: Doing a project in which your focus is on how a particular word (e.g., "like," "just," "really"; Tagliamonte, 2005), figure of speech (e.g., conventional metaphors for depression; McMullen & Conway, 2002), or so-called paralinguistic feature (e.g., laughter; Edwards, 2005) is used and on the functions and possible consequences of various usages has the advantage of narrowing your selection of extracts of talk or text for analysis. However, as with all discursive research, it is important to keep in mind that the context(s) from which you extract specific devices for analysis shapes the uses and functions of these devices. So, although the selection of instances might be more straightforward than in other projects, you still have to be sensitive to the likelihood that instances of the same device will be used differently and will serve different functions depending on the context from which they are derived. For example, you might find that the "depression is to diabetes as antidepressants are to insulin" analogy continues to be used without critique on websites that advertise antidepressants. As a consequence, any conclusions that you draw from your analysis should reflect this context dependence.

Example 2: How "X" Is Constructed

A common focus of discursive psychology is on how a concept, a category of persons, a social practice, or an event is constructed in talk or text. The scope of substantive areas investigated via this focus attests to its salience and versatility. Some examples of foci include (a) health-related topics, such as paranoia (Harper, 1994) or obesity and anorexia nervosa (Whitehead & Kurz, 2008); (b) topics in social psychology, such as otherness (Sakki & Pettersson, 2016), place and national identity (Wallwork & Dixon, 2004), or social categories (e.g., villains and victims; Wood & Rennie, 1994); (c) cultural practices (e.g., infant feeding, Williams et al., 2013; or safer sex, Bowleg et al., 2015); (d) ideologies, such as feminism (Edley & Wetherell, 2001); and (e) social, political, and justice issues, such as climate change (Kurz et al., 2010) and racism (Every & Augoustinos, 2007). In these sorts of studies, researchers are interested in showing how speakers or writers actively put together the meaning(s) of a concept, category, activity, event, or practice through their use of particular linguistic devices and resources.

To provide one version of how you might go about analyzing data that are focused on how "X" is constructed, I draw from a study that one of my former students, Elizabeth Alexander, and I conducted on stories of postpartum depression (PPD) that were published in Canadian and American newspapers between 2008 and 2012 (Alexander & McMullen, 2015). As is often the case with qualitative research, our initial interest in public presentations of PPD, per se, was supplanted by what we found to be two intriguing features of our data set: (a) the publication in 2010, and subsequent wide-spread newspaper coverage, of an academic article by Paulson and Bazemore on prenatal and postnatal depression in fathers and its relation to maternal depression and (b) the frequency of explicit and implicit references to mothering and motherhood and fathering and fatherhood in the stories. These features led us to the following research question: How are constructions of mothering and motherhood and fathering and fatherhood fashioned in newspaper articles on PPD?

Working from a final sample of 20 articles focused on paternal PPD and 75 articles focused on maternal PPD, we first developed a set of key words (e.g., "baby," "child," "little one," "mother," "mom," "father," "dad," "parent," "partner," "spouse," "family," "relationship") to identify extracts for analysis. This list of key words was developed, in part, by our initial generation of what we considered to be relevant terms and, in part, by our gleaning of terms from the multiple readings of our data set. What resulted from the use of these key words was a data set that comprised 175 extracts from articles focused primarily on maternal PPD and 134 extracts from articles focused primarily on paternal PPD, each of which was focused on mothering and motherhood and/or fathering and fatherhood.

We summarized our analytic process as follows:

> We engaged in multiple readings of the extracts, often returning in an iterative fashion to the full versions of the newspaper articles. When engaged in these readings, we paid particular attention to the specific words that were chosen to frame mothering/motherhood and fathering/fatherhood, particularly to the use of category systems, metaphors, stylistic and grammatical features, and rhetorical strategies (Potter & Wetherell, 1987; Wood & Kroger, 2000); to how events, situations, and people were presented through devices such as foregrounding, backgrounding, and presupposing (i.e., assuming their taken-for-grantedness); and to how relationships among the actors were constructed. In addition to focusing on what was present and included, we also paid attention to absences and omissions (Wood & Kroger, 2000). (Alexander & McMullen, 2015, p. 148)

This deceptively straightforward summary glosses over four important points that have to be unpacked. First, extracting segments of text for analysis necessarily takes them out of context. Although I recommend that you preserve the immediate context (i.e., small segments of text that directly precede and follow the extract of interest), it is important that you not lose sight of other segments of the text that might influence how you read a particular extract—hence the importance of iteratively moving between extracts and full texts. Consider Extract 3 which is taken from our data set.

If you extracted only the sentence that begins "A recent survey," you might have focused on the use of an authoritatively supported ("a recent survey") declarative construction of fact regarding societal pressures on women ("pressured to be perfect") not to expose the challenges of being a mother ("lied about parenting"). So, you might have been alerted to two possible constructions: "perfect mothering" and "actual mothering."

EXTRACT 3

The tendency is for moms to gush about how wonderful motherhood is. How rewarding and deliciously amusing and blissful it is. How things couldn't be peachier with their new little best friend. . . . A recent survey . . . found that many mothers lied about parenting because they felt pressured to be perfect. (Withey, 2011, as cited in Alexander & McMullen, 2015, pp. 153–154)

However, including the three pieces of text that precede this sentence as part of the extract—"The tendency is for moms to gush . . . couldn't be peachier with their new little best friend"—enabled us to read this part of the extract as an escalating set of evocative words and phrases that functioned to construct the overly happy mother as a caricature of what might be considered the perfect mother in our culture. Taken as a whole, we saw this extract as using a combination of hyperbole and sarcasm followed by techniques of fact construction as a way of first constructing and then disputing the notion of the perfect mother.

Another extract from this same article further develops the context of the article.

EXTRACT 4

While most new moms aren't prancing around in unitards and tutus, many of us . . . are, like Nina, grappling with the same desire to be faultless. To be the Queen of Mothers. To exclusively breastfeed at all hours with a euphoric grin on our faces. To vigilantly check toys and soaps for potentially hazardous ingredients. To keep that child happy and safe no matter the cost to us. To our sanity. (Withey, 2011, as cited in Alexander & McMullen, 2015, p. 154)

Here, again, you might see a pattern in the oscillating use of both caricature ("prancing around in unitards and tutus," "Queen of Mothers") and hyperbole ("To exclusively breastfeed at all hours with a euphoric grin on our faces") to construct the notion of the perfect mother as folly, followed by a nonfigurative declaration of the negative consequences of this construction ("To keep that child happy and safe no matter the cost to us. To our sanity"). Taking these two extracts together, you might read the context of this article as one of resistance toward the notion of the perfect mother. To reiterate, reading extracts in the context of what immediately and more distally precedes and follows them is important during analysis.

Second, working up how a particular notion, concept, social category, practice, event, and so forth, is constructed requires that you be alert to how various linguistic features, including non-content-related features, are used to put together or frame whatever is of interest to you. For example, consider the following quote "She was just an anxious 'terrible mother' because she couldn't get her newborn to nap" (Zdeb, 2011, as cited in Alexander & McMullen, 2015, p. 151). If you read this sentence for content only, you might see a framing of "terrible mother[ing]" as an inability to accomplish what could be considered everyday tasks of "good mothering" (i.e., getting a newborn to nap). However, the enclosing of "terrible mother" in quotation marks could be read as signaling that this judgment is a societal category that can be questioned and perhaps read as hyperbolic in the context in which it appears. To check whether this initial hypothesis is supported, you would read the entire article to determine whether confirming evidence is present.

Consider another example of how you might attend to the rhetorical power of non–content-related or stylistic features of language use in analyzing how a category, concept, event, practice, and so forth, is constructed. The following extract consists of the opening sentences of an article titled "Fathers, Too, Experience Prenatal and Postnatal Depression" (Roan, 2010, as cited in Alexander & McMullen, 2015).

EXTRACT 5

"They might relish becoming parents, but they can also be unprepared for the infant in their lives. They're sleep-deprived, confused and irritable. They're the fathers" (Roan, 2010, as cited in Alexander & McMullen, 2015, p. 155).

Despite the title of the article, you might wonder, on a first reading of the opening two sentences, to whom the unspecified "they" refers. Is it fathers as named in the title? Is it mothers whom we might characteristically (perhaps stereotypically) think of as desiring to be parents and as experiencing the deleterious effects of caring for infants? What was your reaction when you read the third sentence? And what would you make of the author's explicit naming of "fathers" in the third sentence of this extract? Our reading was that the first two sentences of this extract might function to set up the reader to expect that these sentences are referencing the normative experience of mothers and that the explicit naming of "fathers" in the third sentence serves to jolt the reader out of stereotyped expectations about fatherhood and fathering. As with the previous example, the point here is that you should not ignore what might seem an innocuous feature of language use (in this case, the parallel and repeated use of the unspecified "they" at the beginning of the sentences) or dismiss your reactions to a piece of text or talk. Because we are so accustomed to the norms of the culture(s) within which we reside, it is precisely these features and reactions that can sometimes assist you in recognizing what we often take for granted in how we are constructing a particular concept, category, practice, or event.

In addition, discursive analyses of how "X" is constructed often require that you be alert to culturally available discourses or broad patterns of language use that speakers and writers can draw on and local customs and norms that can be either explicitly or implicitly referenced by speakers or writers. Such awareness can come from your or others' lived experience and your knowledge of what researchers from a variety of disciplinary allegiances have had to say on the topic of your research.

For example, in our readings of our corpus of newspaper articles on PPD, we noticed many instances of what we deemed to be negative characterizing of mothering and motherhood. Being familiar with what has been termed a discourse of the "bad mother" (Ladd-Taylor & Umansky, 1998), we first started to draw together extracts from the articles that included words and phrases that seemed to us to be consistent with this discourse. Examples of our groupings of these words and phrases included explicit references to the presence of negative feelings and/or the absence of positive feelings toward the baby, an emphasis on harm, and an enumeration of an inability to carry out the tasks of mothering. However, we also saw in these extracts often implicit messages about what constituted "good mothering" and how powerfully entrenched in our society is the expectation of motherhood as joy.

Consider the following quote from a mother who was presented as experiencing PPD, along with a brief account of our analytic process: "Saying I am feeling resentment toward my children is a really hard thing to come out and say" (Hill, 2012, as cited in Alexander & McMullen, 2015, p. 152). In this case, we first drew on what particular words denote, specifically "feeling resentment," which signals anger at something considered unjust or wrong. We then drew on our cultural knowledge of possible meanings of the phrase "a really hard thing to come out and say." To do so, we asked ourselves, "What is it about coming out and saying that one resents one's children that makes this disclosure difficult for a mother?" We brainstormed that doing so might carry the risk of feeling ashamed or embarrassed, exposing feelings that should not be made public, or possibly being judged negatively by others. We then inferred that the speaker's framing of feelings of resentment toward her children as difficult to disclose might be due, at least in part, to societal sanctions against such an admission. But then we had to ask ourselves, "Why might such sanctions be referenced in the present context?" Given that these words were presented as having been spoken by a mother, we then reasoned that feeling anger toward one's children out of a sense of having been wronged by them is implicitly connected to the discourse of the "bad mother" in our society because it violates the expectation of unconditional positivity and love that our society has equated with being a "good mother."

This latter claim is, of course, our interpretation of this piece of data. However, as clearly stated by Wiggins (2017), in discursive analysis, it is incumbent on you, as the analyst, to "provide a clear, plausible and insightful interpretation" (p. 135) of your data. Describing, paraphrasing, or assuming that the data "speak for themselves" is insufficient in this kind of work. Although you must ground any interpretation in the data themselves and be explicit when you move beyond your data to make connections to relevant theory and research, it will be up to your audience, in the end, to determine the aptness of your interpretations and connections.

Third, in addition to being alert both to how specific linguistic features are used to construct a particular version of the notion, concept, category, event, process, and so forth, that is of interest to you and to the presence (or absence) of broader discourses on which speakers and writers draw, your analysis might be informed by how items in your data set are structured. In newspaper articles, features of structure can include the form and content of titles, the order in which content is placed in the article, and foregrounding versus backgrounding (the use of certain forms or devices, along with the absence of others). One of the features that struck us in our data set was the frequent referencing of maternal PPD (MPPD) in articles focused on paternal PPD (PPPD). Such referencing occurred prominently in the titles of articles on PPPD. As we stated in our article,

> Some titles, such as "'Baby Blues' are Not Just Women's Domain" (Kirkey, 2010) and "New Dads Hit by Depression as Often as Moms" (Szabo, 2010), referenced MPPD directly via the use of "women" or "moms," whereas others—for example, "Children's Health Matters: Dads Can Have Depression Too" (Anonymous, 2009)—relied on the presumed shared cultural knowledge

that mothers are the implied comparator, as in the use of "too." (Alexander & McMullen, 2015, p. 155)

Paying attention to the titles of the articles alerted us to notions of foregrounding and backgrounding (i.e., what is made more or less prominent in the articles) and to notions of what might be constructed as normative and taken for granted and, in contrast, nonnormative.

Noticing that "women" and "moms" were referenced in the titles of articles on PPPD led us to wonder about the extent to which, and how, fathering or fatherhood was referenced in articles focused on MPPD. What we found was that, whereas mothers were referenced in every article focused on PPPD in our sample, references to fathers or dads occurred in only nine of the 75 articles focused on MPPD. Instead, a notable feature in the articles focused on MPPD was the comparatively greater number of references to "husbands" as opposed to "fathers" or "dads." In the context of partner references, "husbands" were referenced more than twice as often as "fathers" or "dads" (in 22.8% vs. 10.3% of the extracts, respectively). In the context of fewer references to "fathers" or "dads," we argued that references to "husbands" can serve to foreground, perhaps even privilege, the spousal relationship over the parenting relationship, thereby backgrounding and diminishing a focus on the role of fathering in the articles (Alexander & McMullen, 2015, p. 156). Here is an example of how attending to structural features of your data (and even thinking quantitatively) can inform you about what is present and what is (comparatively) absent from how your focus of interest is constructed.

Fourth, the structure of our data set itself facilitated the adoption of a comparative analytic stance (see Wood & Kroger, 2000, p. 94). Specifically, our corpus of newspaper articles on PPD provided us with the advantage of having what could be considered two data sets—articles on MPPD and articles on PPPD. Having articles with these complementary but different foci enabled us to direct our attention to how mothering or motherhood and fathering or fatherhood were constructed in relation to each other.

I have already alluded to some of the contrasting ways we thought about our data as the project proceeded—for example, that mothers and women were often referenced both in the titles and in the text of articles on PPPD, whereas the converse was rarely, if ever, the case. However, what first alerted us to the importance of adopting a comparative stance was what we eventually came to see as the sharp contrast between the well-articulated expectations of what constitutes "bad" (or poor or failing) mothering and "good" mothering and the ill-articulated expectations of what constitutes fathering. Consider the following extracts.

EXTRACT 6

Women who become depressed after childbirth not only battle their feelings, but have the added guilt of feeling that they're failing as mothers. They may feel emotionally detached from their babies and react negatively to a fussy, sick or crying child. (Anonymous, 2011a, as cited in Alexander & McMullen, 2015, p. 149)

EXTRACT 7

"I didn't feel the glow of sunlight with my baby, being blissed-out as I was sitting and rocking her . . . I felt like I was supposed to love [her] more. I felt I was a bad mother because I wasn't doing it right" (Hunter, 2010, as cited in Alexander & McMullen, 2015, p. 152).

In these two extracts, we noted the following features: (a) the presence of what can be considered discourses or broad patterns of ways of talking about mothers (i.e., as "failing" or "bad") and (b) the presence of particular instantiations of these discourses in the form of exemplars of what constitutes failed mothering ("feel[ing] emotionally detached from their babies and react[ing] negatively to a fussy, sick or crying child") and bad mothering ("I didn't feel the glow of sunlight with my baby, being blissed-out as I was sitting and rocking her . . . I felt like I was supposed to love [her] more"). On the basis of these observations, we argued that the existence of well-defined societal expectations for "good" mothering—and, hence, what, by extension, constitutes "failing" or "bad" mothering—is linked to subsequent claims of self-blaming on the part of mothers.

Now consider the following extracts.

EXTRACT 8

We are expecting dads to be more involved in parenting than we ever have before. . . . Most dads are welcoming of that, but they don't have any models about what a dad is supposed to do. That creates uncertainty, and that uncertainty can lead to anxiety and depression. (Roan, 2010, as cited in Alexander & McMullen, 2015, p. 158)

EXTRACT 9

"For expectant dads, you can tell them all you want about what's going to happen, and they won't get it until it happens to them" (Bothum, 2010, as cited in Alexander & McMullen, 2015, p. 159).

If you adopted a comparative stance, you might note that, in Extract 8, fathers, too, are cast as the product of gender-based societal structuring but in a sympathetic light—they want to be involved but do not know how ("Most dads are welcoming of [being more involved in parenting], but they don't have any models about what a dad is supposed to do"). Being constructed as not knowing what to do through no fault of one's own stands in sharp contrast to the well-formulated discourses of the "failing" or "bad" mother and the claims to self-blame that ensued. In Extract 9, you might see a slightly different variation of the link between expectations and consequent behavior. In this case, expectations of what constitutes fathering are framed as available, but unattended to. Again, however, fathers are cast in a sympathetic light by being constructed as naive and unsuspecting, and self-blaming for not living up to societal expectations is absent.

During our various analytic forays into the data for this project, we kept in mind the importance of formulating an argument about the meaning and significance of our analytic claims. Although discursive projects do not always lend themselves to a single or unitary argument about meaning and significance, we drew together the strands of our analytic claims about how motherhood or mothering and fatherhood or fathering were constructed in our corpus of newspaper articles into one distinction. Specifically, bringing together our claims that (a) fathers were put in the background in articles focused on MPPD, whereas mothers were kept in the foreground in articles focused on PPPD, and (b) mothering and motherhood were constructed as deeply imbued with expectations, whereas fathering and fatherhood were characterized by the unavailability of or inattention to clearly specified expectations, we argued that our corpus of data was a site in which mothering and motherhood remained primary and normative, and fatherhood and fathering was "othered."

In summary, when you are interested in pursuing a discursive project that is focused on how "X" is constructed, your analysis will benefit from bringing to bear the following:

- your articulated (pre-) conceptions of "X" and of how the context from which you will derive your data (e.g., popular culture, research interviews, everyday conversations, autobiographies, blogs, focus groups, social media, magazine or newspaper articles) might shape your analysis;

- your familiarity with the language in which you are working (e.g., vocabulary, sentence structure, grammatical constructions);

- your knowledge of the range of linguistic devices available to speakers and writers (e.g., words, tropes, stylistic features, paralinguistic cues);

- your sensitivity to the significance of, for example, particular choices of words and word combinations, grammatical forms, stylistic features, and paralinguistic cues;

- your ability to think in terms of how speakers and writers are using particular linguistic resources, the possible functions of such uses, and their potential effects;

- your willingness to challenge the taken-for-granted and to make the familiar strange;

- your diligence in linking your analytic claims (interpretations) to evidence (data); and

- your ability to formulate an argument about the meaning and/or significance of your analytic claims.

Example 3: What Social Actions Are Being Performed

As with research questions related to how "X" is constructed, an interest in what speakers and writers are doing with their use of language draws attention to a central feature of how discourse can be understood in discursive psychology—that is, as a form of social action (Potter, 2003). Here, the focus is on how people use discursive devices, resources, and strategies (e.g., categories, metaphors, narratives, grammatical forms, consensus, management of stake) to carry out particular actions. These actions can include everyday activities, such as telling, requesting, commanding, complimenting, blaming, apologizing, inviting, sympathizing, refusing, scolding, colluding, absolving, reassuring, and so forth.

Of course, such actions take place in particular contexts. Consequently, the actions that are the focus of analyses undertaken within the framework of discursive psychology are often cast in more particularized terms. For example, Coates and Wade (2007) analyzed accounts of personalized violence from a perpetrator and persons in authority (e.g., a psychiatrist, a judge) and showed how four discursive operations (or actions)—concealing violence, obfuscating perpetrators' responsibility, concealing victims' resistance, and blaming and pathologizing victims—were used to produce inaccurate versions of events. In this case, the framing of these four actions can be seen as clearly specific to the topic of the research—accounts of personalized violence.

Another way of drawing attention to the notion of language use as contextualized social action is to pair the notion of "doing" with a familiar noun or colloquialism. For example, in a study of celebrities' talk during radio interviews, I labeled one of the social actions being performed by the celebrities as "doing modesty" (McMullen, 2005). In this case, a familiar noun, "modesty," is turned into an action by prefacing it with "doing," which turns it from a behavior or characteristic of a person into a social action. Discursive researchers have also drawn attention to their focus on a social action by naming it with a familiar colloquialism. For example, Lofgren et al. (2015) named the action performed by clinical psychologists as they discursively constructed the notion of mental health as "doing fence-sitting." Similarly, Horne and Wiggins (2009) used the phrase "doing being 'on the edge'" to describe how participants in an online forum worked to manage the dilemma of being authentically suicidal. These examples are intended to sensitize you not only to the importance of thinking about language use as the performance of social actions in particular contexts but also to the significance of studying the everyday—often taken-for-granted—actions we routinely perform.

To illustrate how you can keep a focus on what speakers or writers are doing with language, I use an example from a set of interviews I conducted with persons who were prescribed an antidepressant for a condition other than depression or anxiety (McMullen, 2016). This study was part of a larger project on how evidence-based practice with regard to the use of antidepressants is constructed. As is not uncommon in my research, the first question I became intrigued with after familiarizing myself with the interview data was not about evidence-based practice, but rather was formed from my observation that all the interviewees oriented to and took up the category "depression" without my posing any explicit questions about it. After deciding to pursue the question of how the interviewees and I discursively managed talk of "depression" in the context of an interview about the use of antidepressants for a condition other than depression or anxiety, I extracted all segments of talk from the interviews in which talk of depression occurred. As I worked with these extracts, I looked for patterns in the data and kept returning to the question "What are the speakers doing?" I eventually labeled what I saw as the primary discursive move being engaged in as "decoupling the relation between an antidepressant and a diagnosis of (characterological or clinical) depression." My framing of this move in these terms is an example of how the analyst can make interpretive claims and ascribe meaning to what speakers or writers are doing with language. To illustrate how I saw this move being accomplished, I then focused on three specific actions I claimed the interview participants used to decouple "antidepressants" and "depression": (a) directly or indirectly denying one was characterologically or clinically (as opposed to situationally) depressed, (b) differentiating the nature of one's distress from depression, and (c) reconstructing the antidepressant.

Let us consider two extracts from this study as a way of illustrating, among other points, how you can focus on what actions are being performed by the speakers' or writers' use of language and be alert to patterns in the data. The first extract is from an interview with a woman who was prescribed antidepressants for symptoms associated with multiple sclerosis (MS), primarily fatigue. It is taken from an early part of the interview in which the interviewee is talking about having first been prescribed Prozac immediately after receiving the diagnosis of MS. "P" refers to the interviewee, and "L" to the interviewer.

EXTRACT 10

1. P07: . . . and I was never on a very high dose for the Prozac it was always an extremely low dose

2. L. Okay

3. P07: and it was just (.) enough to help with the symptoms of fatigue

4. L: Okay and for you was there any (.) you mentioned earlier that that it was clear that it was for fatigue because you didn't feel <u>depressed</u> at that time (.) was that↑

5. P07: Well I just didn't have <u>time</u> (chuckle) to be depressed

6. L: Didn't have time to be depressed (.) that's right

7. P07: I was too busy I mean I was working full time and I had a young daughter

At a general level, you might read this extract as the interviewee explaining how she knows that the antidepressant was not prescribed for depression. Articulating what you generally see as going on in a segment of talk or text is a good first analytic step and helps keep you focused on the action orientation, on what actions are being accomplished with the discourse (Wiggins, 2017, p. 14). In addition, as noted by Wood and Kroger (2000), stating what might seem as "the obvious" can draw your attention to actions that might otherwise go unnoticed.

With this general sense of what is going on in mind, you might then ask how, specifically, is the action of explaining that the antidepressant was not prescribed for depression accomplished? Let us consider the first line of Extract 10: "and I was never on a very high dose for the Prozac it was always an extremely low dose." One way of reading this statement—and the one that was most compelling to me—is that the interviewee, through the use of extreme case formulation ("never," "always," "extremely"; Edwards & Potter, 1992), is constructing the way in which the antidepressant was used in her case as unusual. By drawing on my knowledge of how anti-depressants are often used to treat depression—beginning with a low dose and increasing until a positive effect is achieved—as well as on the inter-viewee's statement about how antidepressants are prescribed for depression ("They start you off low and bring you up until you are getting a positive effect"), which occurred just before this extract, I reasoned that, in con-structing her prescription as a low, nonincreasing dose, the interviewee's talk can be read as differentiating it from the typical way antidepressants are used to treat depression. Here, I am making an interpretation and being explicit about it so the reader can judge its reasonableness.

In the third line of this extract, the interviewee continues her framing of how the antidepressant was used ("and it was just (.) enough to help with the symptoms of fatigue"). The use of "just (.) enough" again emphasizes the lowness of the dosage, which, when followed by "to help with the symptoms of fatigue," further marks the limits of the use of the antidepressant in her case. Although "the symptoms of fatigue" could be taken as evidence of depression, the interviewee had explicitly mentioned in an earlier part of the interview that such symptoms are well known to be a primary feature of MS. Hence, claiming to be treated for fatigue without it being an indi-cator of depression is plausible in this context. With my focus kept on what the interviewee is doing, I then labeled this strategy as "reconstructing the antidepressant" in the service of "decoupling the relation between an anti-depressant and a diagnosis of (characterological or clinical) depression."

Several reflexive and analytic moves are at play here. First, the reflexive moves: (a) I have emphasized that this reading of the first line of Extract 10 is my reading, and although you might have a different reading, it is important that you provide evidence for your particular reading, that you link your analytic claims to the use of particular linguistic devices or resources in the talk or text and that you be explicit as to how you are interpreting the function(s) served by such devices or resources; and (b) I have acknowledged that the analyst brings into the analysis differing sets of knowledge about the topic at hand—in this case, my familiarity with how antidepressants are typically prescribed for depression. These differing sets of knowledge will influence the sense you make of your data. Acknowledging what you bring to your analysis is a recognition that there is no one correct interpretation or set of conclusions in discursive research and that different analysts are likely to produce at least somewhat different interpretations or sets of conclusions. Now, the analytic moves: (a) I have linked the interviewee's use of a particular linguistic device (e.g., extreme case formulations) to my claim that the interviewee is constructing the use of antidepressants in her case as unusual, so I am showing you (the reader) the evidence on which I am making my analytic claim; and (b) I am constantly thinking about what the speaker—in this case, the interviewee—is doing, so my focus is on naming the social actions that I see being performed in the talk.

Now, let us consider the remainder of Extract 10 and how I saw it as evidence of another discursive action, directly or indirectly denying one was characterologically depressed. Note, first, that my clarifying query in line 4 resurrects a possible connection made earlier in the interview between the use of antidepressants and depression ("You mentioned earlier that that it was clear that it was for fatigue because you didn't feel <u>depressed</u> at that time (.) was that↑"). The interviewee then responds in line 5 by correcting my version of events ("Well I just didn't have <u>time</u> (chuckle) to be depressed") through emphasizing not having "<u>time</u> to be depressed." In line 7, she then asserts the factuality of this claim ("I was too busy I mean I was working full time and I had a young daughter") through the use of two identity categories—full-time worker and mother of a young child—and the entitlement (Antaki & Widdicombe, 1998)—"too busy"—that follows from the combination of these identity categories. Taking the interviewee's disclaimer regarding being depressed, along with her use of this combination of identity categories and its entitlement, I interpreted the interviewee as positioning herself as someone who pushes through adversity—an interpretation that is bolstered by a subsequent claim by the interviewee ("Yeah I just didn't have time I had to push everything back push everything off")—implying that if she were to be depressed, it would be because circumstances in her life (not her character) enabled or allowed her to be depressed.

In this part of the analysis, I again drew on my preexisting knowledge, specifically of the major discourses or ways of talking about depression that are available to speakers and writers in parts of the Western world. These discourses are typically framed as etiological models and include (a) biomedical understandings (depression as a symptom-defined illness caused by chemical imbalances in the brain and/or by genetic heritability), (b) social understandings (depression as an outcome of deprivation or difficult life circumstances), and (c) psychological understandings (depression as a consequence of faulty cognitive processes and the presence of particular characterological features of the individual, sometimes in combination with stressful life events). I also again linked my analytic claims about how the interviewee was positioning herself as a person—one who "pushes through adversity"—to the linguistic devices used by her to accomplish this construction. Finally, I again kept my focus on the social action being performed and argued that the interviewee was implicitly denying that she was a characterologically depressed person who needed a prescription for an antidepressant.

One additional point about the analysis of this extract warrants reiterating. You might have noticed that part of my attention was directed to my contribution to the interaction in this extract, specifically to my redirecting the focus of the interview in line 4 to the interviewee's earlier talk about the antidepressant being prescribed for fatigue and not for depression. As I mentioned earlier, the connection of antidepressants to depression was not a focus of conversation I initiated in these interviews. However, if the interviewee introduced this focus, I followed up on it, as evidenced in this extract. Because every conversation is a coconstructed process, it is important to be aware of the contributions of all speakers and how these contributions shape the conversation. Focusing just on what interviewees are doing with language is likely to lead to an impoverished analysis.

Now, let us consider a second extract that comes from an interview with a woman who was prescribed an antidepressant for the sequelae of a concussion. This extract follows from the interviewee's talk about how she did not think of this medication as an antidepressant because she was informed that it was now used for pain control and not for the treatment of depression.

If you were already alerted to the action of "reconstructing the antidepressant" by noting its presence in Extract 10, you might notice that the interviewee in Extract 11 engages in a similar action in lines 3 and 5. Specifically, this interviewee also invokes and emphasizes the use of a low dose of the medication ("<u>minimum</u> 150 milligrams . . . and you're taking 10") to argue against it being used to treat depression. So, here marks the

EXTRACT 11

1. PO2: And I would say I'm on a drug that originally was used for an antidepressant back in the day and it's now used to manage pain control

2. ...

3. PO2: And I think when they [healthcare providers] said to me (.) um (.) to manage for antidepressant you know we prescribed <u>minimum</u> 150 milligrams

4. L: Yes

5. PO2: and you're taking 10

6. L: Yes

7. PO2: They were- everybody was <u>very</u> like (.) um open and upfront about that too to

8. L: Yeah, yeah

9. PO2: I think to make me feel uh reassured that (.) if if it was an antidepressant 10 milligrams wasn't going to do anything for that

10. L: Yeah

11. PO2: right↑

12. L: Yeah. So again it can, it is, you sort of felt that they were very clear although maybe not (.) explicit about wanting to defuse any notion that this would be for depression↑

13. PO2: Right. In saying that↑ I'm <u>not</u> um (5) ○>how do I wanna say this<○ I, I, I, it wasn't that I didn't think that a mild traumatic brain injury could cause some depression symptoms right↑

observation of a pattern in the data that can alert you to something that is possibly worth analyzing.

However, the interviewee in Extract 11 goes much further than citing only a low dose as evidence of the medication not being used to treat depression. In the opening two lines of this extract, she further reconstructs the antidepressant she was prescribed through four discursive moves. First, she uses the generic category "drug" rather than the specific category "antidepressant," which can serve to separate her prescribed medication from the category of medications labeled as antidepressants. Second, she separates the medication's present use from its former use as an antidepressant ("originally was used for"). Third, she frames its use as an antidepressant as outdated ("back in the day"). Fourth, she constructs its modern and current use as not for depression ("now used to manage pain control"). By analyzing these moves, you can not only show how the action of "reconstructing the antidepressant" is further nuanced by this interviewee but also can illustrate one of the major assumptions of the discursive perspective—recognizing variability as a feature of discourse (Wood & Kroger, 2000, p. 10).

Now, let us focus on the last few turns of talk in this extract (lines 9 through 13). Here is what I had to say about them, beginning with the interviewee's turn (line numbers altered from the original).

> However, her account begins to waver, as is evident by her repeated use of "if" (l. [line] 9) and of the uncertainty marker "right↑" (l. 11; Wood & Kroger, 2000), when she opens up the possibility that the medication might have been used as an antidepressant. The interviewee's response to my restatement (l. 13) suggests some trouble with regard to the topic of depression as is evidenced by her false starts, rather lengthy pause, and quieter and quicker self-talk ("I'm <u>not</u> um (5) °>how do I wanna say this<° I, I, I,"), indirect affirming through the use of double negatives ("it wasn't that I didn't think"), and use again of the uncertainty marker "right." Using the indefinite article "a" ("a mild traumatic brain injury"; l. 13), as opposed to personalizing the possible connection of her own mild traumatic brain injury to depression and referencing "depression symptoms" rather than "depression," both normalizes the causal relation of the injury to features of depression and enables her to distance herself from actually claiming that she experienced diagnosable depression. In this instance, the interviewee cautiously raises the possibility that the circumstances of a mild traumatic brain injury (which she later in the interview specified as the social isolation required for recovery) could lead to symptoms associated with depression. So, to distance herself from a diagnosis of depression that requires an antidepressant, she reconstructs the antidepressant, separates symptoms from the diagnosis, and normalizes these symptoms as secondary to a concussion. (McMullen, 2016, p. 153)

Here, again, I see a pattern in the repetition of the action of "directly or indirectly denying that one was characterologically or clinically depressed" that was evident in Extract 10. Specifically, in this turn of talk in Extract 11, any indication of depression is reduced to symptoms shared with the sequelae of a concussion and, consequently, situationally based. Although how the interviewee in Extract 11 goes about distancing herself from a diagnosis of depression that requires an antidepressant is different from how the interviewee in Extract 10 does so, I argue that the broad discursive action is the same.

My purpose for including my analysis of the last few turns of talk in Extract 11 is to underscore two additional analytic points. One, in fashioning your analysis, you can draw on segments of talk or text not included in the particular extract you are analyzing. In this case, my turn of talk indirectly references a previous segment of the interview in which the interviewee had constructed the message from health care providers as being clear that they were not prescribing an antidepressant because they thought she was experiencing depression. In addition, I directly reference in my analysis a later segment of the interview in which the interviewee explicitly states that she experienced the effects of social isolation during her recovery. In drawing on such segments, you can lend validity to your analysis if you inform your readers that you are relying on some material that is outside of what is available to them.

Two, a small segment of text or talk can sometimes require a lengthy analysis. Although I do not always bring paralinguistic features into my analysis of a segment of talk or focus on linguistic features such as word repetitions or infrequently used sentence structures as conversation analysts would, I do so when my interpretative claims warrant it. In hearing and reading the last turn of talk of the interviewee in Extract 11, I sensed some trouble in her taking up of the link between antidepressants and depression that I had made in my immediately preceding turn of talk. To convey to the reader what it was in the interviewee's talk that I understood as trouble, I deemed it necessary to link her use of specific features with my analytic claims. If your claims necessitate a lengthy analysis, take the time (and space) required. Making your argument with a robust analysis of a short piece of text or talk is much preferred to trying to do so via a thin analysis of many extracts.

One final comment with respect to focusing on the actions being performed in talk or text: Speakers and writers will almost always engage in many more actions than you will focus on in your analysis. So, you will have to decide which actions inform your research question(s) and, consequently, will be the source of your analysis, and you will have to ignore the others (perhaps until you fashion other research questions that can be informed from your data).

Whose Analysis?

Researchers who use qualitative methodologies and methods of data collection, generation, and analysis sometimes engage others (e.g., members of a research team, stakeholders) in the process of analyzing data. Purposes for doing so can include a desire to increase the accuracy of the analysis through achieving consensus across analysts, a belief that an analysis benefits from multiple perspectives on the data and an acknowledgment of the importance of stakeholders' knowledge of what the data mean. Although the desirability or necessity of achieving consensus across analysts would not be consistent with the constructionist epistemological orientation of discourse analysis, some discursive analysts might engage others in various ways during the analytic process. For example, I occasionally have brought segments of my analysis, usually a few extracts and my claims and interpretations, to my research team meetings. I have done so not to achieve consensus or engage in a group analysis, but rather to assess whether the logic of my analytic claims and interpretations is clear, convincing, and generative. That is, do others think I have effectively warranted my claims by linking them to evidence in the talk or text, persuasively argued my interpretation of the patterns I have worked up, and contributed something useful to our understanding of the topic? Consulting others—particularly those from different locations and disciplinary stances—about connections they might make between your data and broader discourses can also be helpful. However, I undertake almost all my analytic work on my own, beginning with generating or collecting the data, immersing myself in them, extracting a subset for formal workup, writing the analysis, and preparing the conference presentation, manuscript, book chapter, or other form of communication. My point here is that there is no single, correct way of conducting your analysis. If you decide to use others in the process of analyzing your data, just be clear about your reason for doing so and be epistemologically consistent in your practices. If you decide to go solo, do not think there is anything wrong with this decision. Remember that your audiences, including research supervisors, reviewers, readers, and stakeholders, will be the final arbiters of the quality, meaningfulness, and significance of your work.

CONCLUDING COMMENTS ON ANALYZING YOUR DATA

Working with discursive data requires you to confront a paradox: Although the process of analysis could be interminable, you must conclude it at some point. You will get a sense of this interminability if you revisit your data set after working up a selection of extracts or revisit your analysis of a particular selection of extracts. In either case, you will almost invariably see something new that could be analyzed or different ways of writing your existing analysis. Deciding whether you are ready to conclude your analysis might be aided by considering questions such as

- Have I kept my (finalized) research question(s) in mind as I worked with my data?
- Have I engaged in multiple and varied readings of the data I have chosen to analyze?
- Have I paid attention to the links between the use of discursive devices and resources and the possible functions being served by this use?
- Have I linked my analytic claims to evidence in the data?
- Have I provided my interpretation of these analytic claims?
- Am I satisfied that I have exhausted what I need to say to present a convincing argument to readers?

Answering in the affirmative to questions of this sort can indicate that, for now, you are ready to stop analyzing your data.

5 DISSEMINATING YOUR RESEARCH

Although it is customary to think of disseminating one's research in the form of a conference presentation, journal article, or book chapter, discursive researchers are increasingly turning to additional practices and outlets (e.g., arts-based approaches, social media, policy documents) as ways of reaching diverse audiences and broadening the impact of their work. These different forms of dissemination can often work in complementary, even synergistic, ways. I encourage you to think expansively and creatively about notions of audience and about ways of disseminating your research and the messages you want to convey.

PREPARING A MANUSCRIPT FOR PUBLICATION IN A JOURNAL

One way to develop a sense of how to write a journal-style manuscript based on a discursive analysis is to read several already-published articles. As mentioned previously, Appendix A includes a few examples of articles I consider to be good illustrations of how to present discursive work. Before beginning to write your manuscript, however, it is a good idea to determine

https://doi.org/10.1037/0000220-005
Essentials of Discursive Psychology, by L. M. McMullen

which journal is best suited to your work. Journals that are more specialized to discourse analysis might not require the level of detailed introduction to discursive psychology that is necessary in a general journal that has a more diverse readership. In any case, you should acquaint yourself with the kinds of discursively oriented articles that have recently been published in particular journals to make an initial judgment about a journal's suitability for your work. In addition, you should familiarize yourself with the instructions to authors with regard to format and style and follow them closely.

General Structure

You will find that work published in the form of a journal article generally follows a standard format that, in many instances, adheres to the rules and guidelines contained in the *Publication Manual of the American Psychological Association* (American Psychological Association, 2020), which is further supplemented by the Journal Article Reporting Standards for Qualitative Research (Levitt et al., 2018). Although the title and abstract of the article are typically the reader's first encounter with your work, I often leave the writing of them until after I have completed the full body of the manuscript. Your title should capture in a few words both the topical and analytic focus of your work. This dual focus is often achieved by using key words or phrases, either from the analyst's workup of the extracts or the data set, coupled with a few words that encapsulate the substance of the study. For example, Bowleg et al.'s (2015) title "Responsible Men, Blameworthy Women: Black Heterosexual Men's Discursive Constructions of Safer Sex and Masculinity" tells the reader that the analysis is focused on how safer sex and masculinity (the general topic) is discursively constructed (the analytic focus) in a particular context (by Black heterosexual male speakers) and provides a hint as to what to expect from the analysis (that it focuses on discourses of Black heterosexual men's responsibility and on the positioning of women as blameworthy).

The abstract usually follows the title and is a longer, but similarly condensed, version of your study. It typically begins with a sentence or two in which you orient the reader to the topic and what we presently know about it, followed by another sentence or two in which you articulate your research focus or question and the rationale for posing it in light of what we already know or do not know. You should then inform your reader of your choices with respect to methodology, data sources, methods of data generation and collection, and methods of data analysis, followed by a brief account of the outcome of your analyses in relation to your research question(s). The abstract typically concludes with a statement or two on the theoretical, conceptual, and/or practical implications and applications of your analytic outcomes.

The introduction and literature review for a discursive study can take many forms and can draw on empirical, theoretical, and conceptual understandings and gaps derived from a variety of sources, including qualitative and quantitative literature from inside and outside the discipline of psychology, your critical consideration of relevant grey literature, and cultural observations and trends. It is important that you use such sources to formulate an argument for the significance and relevance of taking a discursive approach to addressing the question(s) that you derive from these sources.

This setting up of your study is typically followed by a section that I often title "Methodology and Methods." If you have not already briefly outlined your ontological and epistemological stances in your introduction and literature review, you can begin this section with such a statement. Although some readers of your work will understand that discursive work often proceeds from a constructionist or critical realist stance, not all will. Consequently, I continue to include an explicit statement on my ontological and epistemological grounding. In this section, you should also include details on your methodology, data source(s), methods of data collection and generation (including recruitment strategies and participants if you are using methods such as interviews or focus groups) and extract selection, and methods of data analysis.

Because discursive work demands that you show the reader how you are linking evidence (data) and analytic claims, it is not uncommon for the traditional analysis (see the following section for an explanation on the use of this term) and discussion sections to be combined. Doing so gives you the freedom to explicate how you are making sense of and interpreting the data you have chosen to analyze. In other words, you can take the reader inside how you have come to understand the data. This section of the manuscript is often the longest because it usually includes verbatim extracts of data, a detailed analysis of each extract involving the linking of the use of specific discursive devices and resources to your analytic claims about what such use is accomplishing, and your interpretation of the possible consequences of these accomplishments.

Implications and applications of your analysis, as well as questions for future research, can be interwoven in the analysis and discussion section or set apart as a separate section. Rather than ending your manuscript with a statement of the limitations of your research, which are often articulated in terms of its context, I recommend that you remind the reader of the context of your study wherever appropriate throughout your manuscript. Doing so can assist your reader in engaging in a process of analogical generalizability (Smaling, 2003)—an assessment of which aspects of your analysis are and are not analogous, or do or do not apply, to other contexts—and has the potential to stimulate ideas for future research.

Remember that all manuscripts, regardless of their reliance on quantitative or qualitative methodologies, are narratives. They are written in ways that tell a story. For example, details of the existing literature are emphasized or deemphasized both in the introduction and discussion and conclusion, depending on their relevance to the story you want to tell. Similarly, your choice of extracts to include in the manuscript (you will almost always have more than space allows) and the order in which you place these extracts should fit with the narrative you are developing. I recommend that you choose extracts to illustrate variations in the substance of your inquiry and that you order extracts from familiar, taken-for-granted knowledge to the novel, surprising, or provocative. In doing so, you can build tension and intrigue into your narrative.

Writing the Manuscript

Although being aware of the typical format of a manuscript is useful, it does not tell you how to write the manuscript. The main challenge often experienced by those who are new to discursive research is to write in a way that is consistent with one's epistemological stance. This challenge can be particularly acute for students and new researchers who have been trained solely in methodologies that are based in an objectivist epistemology and who are unfamiliar with stances such as constructionism. In this case, it is necessary to abandon the language of hypothesis testing and factors–outcomes and embrace a new vocabulary of, for example, constructions, accounts, and claims, and explicitly recognize the situated nature of one's research, including your impact on the project. Learning to write discursive-based manuscripts with epistemological consistency is akin, in many ways, to learning a new (and, sometimes, quite foreign) language. It takes time and practice.

To sensitize you to this issue of how to write your manuscript, I provide a list of some of the most frequent slippages I have encountered.

- *Imprecise or incorrect use of language.* As mentioned earlier, the borrowing of language that is suitable to an objectivist epistemology is not an uncommon slippage. Typical examples include the use of "findings," which implies that your analysis has uncovered something that exists in the data in and of themselves and apart from your meaning-making work as an analyst. I use "analysis" instead. Similar examples include "discovery" or "emergence," which also imply that meaning exists apart from the analyst's constructions. In addition, reliance on words such as "factors" or "variables," unless invoked by speakers or writers and deemed worthy of analysis, is not typically consistent with a discursive analysis because the goal is not to test for cause–effect relations. The frequent use of "data collection" rather than "data selection" or "data generation" is another common misstep. Although "data collection" might be an appropriate descriptor for those rare instances in which one is using all the preexisting data that exist on a topic, "data selection," which signifies an active set of choices on the part of the researcher, and "data generation," which signifies the active involvement of the researcher in the coming-into-being of the data, are more appropriate terms.

- *Lapsing into language that turns accounts into reality.* A frequent mistake in work that is grounded in a constructionist epistemology (but sometimes not a critical realist stance) is to take what is contained in talk or text as a statement of reality rather than as a version or account. For example, if you were presenting your analysis of how interviewees talked about the etiology of their depression, and one of your interviewees stated that his depression was genetically based, you would say, "Tom's account of his depression is as a genetically based condition" rather than, "Tom's depression is a genetically based condition."

- *Lapsing into the language of psychological constructs.* Unless invoked by the speakers or writers whose talk or text you are analyzing, using terms such as "perceptions," "opinions," "beliefs," "attitudes," "experiences," "personality," and so forth, in your analysis and interpretations is inconsistent with a constructionist epistemology in the context of discursive psychology. As mentioned in Chapter 1, these terms have come to denote structures that exist independently of language; as such, using them is inconsistent with the constructionist notion that we have access only to language, not to underlying psychological structures.

- *Making statements of causality that are neither in the data nor acknowledged as an interpretation.* When discussing one's analysis, it is important not to overstep what can be claimed. As noted earlier, if speakers and writers have invoked causal connections and you have deemed them a construction worthy of analysis, the referencing of such language is warranted. However, if you make causal connections beyond your data, be careful to acknowledge them as interpretations. Do not casually use phrases such as "X leads to Y" or "As a result of X, Y . . ."

- *Relying on notions of statistical (sample to population) generalizability to acknowledge the limitations of small samples.* Because discursive analysis recognizes the context boundedness of data and data analysis and because the aim is not to generalize one's analysis to a population, statements about the limitations of small samples are inappropriate. Instead, make suggestions for how an understanding of your topic or research question(s) might be enhanced by analyzing another set of data drawn from theoretically, conceptually, or otherwise applicable contexts.

BEYOND THE MANUSCRIPT

In outlining the general structure and writing style of a manuscript for a discursive study, I want to be clear that my purpose is not to be prescriptive. Although the journal manuscript is familiar to many of us, it is not the only format for communicating discursive research. Books and book chapters are also quite common modes of communication and can provide greater flexibility than a typical journal manuscript. For example, the work on women and depression I did with Janet Stoppard began as an article in a special issue in *Canadian Psychology* (McMullen, 1999) and then was adapted and rewritten as a book chapter that would be accessible to lay audiences (McMullen, 2003).

In addition, innovative forms of dissemination or knowledge translation, such as arts-based approaches (e.g., a 2018 special issue of *Qualitative Research in Psychology*; Chamberlain et al., 2018), are increasingly challenging qualitative researchers, including discursive analysts (see Gergen & Gergen, 2018), to think beyond the traditional manuscript and book chapter. These approaches can include, for example, presenting your work as a poem, short story, monologue or dialogue, or dramatic performance. These innovations can both complement the more traditional ways in which scholarly research is disseminated and democratize the communication of scientific research.

Although the traditional format of a conference presentation is another option for disseminating your work, it, too, is being challenged by other approaches. For example, although typically undertaken as a competition, the 3-minute thesis, which requires students to explain their research in 180 seconds in language that is appropriate to a nonspecialist audience (https://threeminutethesis.uq.edu.au/about), is a good reminder that we should be able to encapsulate the nub of our research in ways that are accessible to different audiences. The point here is that reaching various audiences in ways that have an impact beyond impact factors is an important part of communicating your research.

6 WHAT CONSTITUTES GOOD DISCURSIVE RESEARCH?

What practices can assist you in producing good discursive research? What criteria should others use to judge the quality of your work? Although these two questions are interrelated, answers to the latter one have often been contentious for discursive analysts. Since the beginning of the present-day reemergence of qualitative inquiry in the discipline of psychology, researchers have been interested in specifying indicators of or criteria for assessing the quality of work that is produced from such inquiry. A few of the many examples of these lists of indicators or criteria include Stiles (1993), Elliott et al. (1999), S. J. Tracy (2010), and Levitt et al. (2017). One of the problems with some of these lists is that they do not recognize the diversity of qualitative methodologies and philosophical assumptions that constitute the field of qualitative inquiry. The most obvious mismatch for discursive analysts is that many of the indicators or criteria that these lists comprise (e.g., representativeness of a sample, member checking, consensus among multiple coders, perspective management, triangulation, relational ethics) are more suited to epistemologies other than a constructionist stance (see Reicher, 2000, for a critique of the notion that a single set of standards for evaluating all forms of qualitative research is a worthy endeavor).

https://doi.org/10.1037/0000220-006
Essentials of Discursive Psychology, by L. M. McMullen

If traditional notions of reliability (repeatability or replicability of research) and validity (correctness of analysis) associated with objectivist research do not apply to constructionist, discursive research, what, then, are the practices and standards that can assist you in producing good discursive work? As articulated by Wood and Kroger (2000) and by Wetherell (1998), your work should be guided by criteria such as *documentation, demonstration, plausibility, coherence,* and *fruitfulness.*

DOCUMENTATION

Documentation (or what has also been termed "transparency"; Wiggins, 2017, p. 136) refers to keeping track of your decisions with regard to the planning, design, and execution of your study and rationales for these decisions and to informing your audience of these decisions and rationales. You should make visible your responses and justifications to questions such as, "Why did I frame my research question(s) in the way I did, and what impact might this framing have had on what I produced?" "How and why did I decide to use particular data-generating or collecting methods in light of my research question(s), and what were the possible impacts of these decisions on the data that were available to me for analysis?" "How did I engage with my data?" "What analytic strategies did I use?" "Which discursive patterns did I decide to work up, and why?" Concerning yourself with these questions not only will enable you to articulate the context of your study but also has the potential to assure your audience that you have carefully deliberated on the many features of your study.

DEMONSTRATION

Although including extracts of data that support one's analytic claims is a feature of many qualitative methodologies, analysts who adopt the perspective of discursive psychology do not assume that the connections between an extract and one's claims are self-evident. That is, they do not make claims about their understanding of a piece of talk or text and then insert an extract of data without further explicitly linking features of the talk or text to their claims. Rather, discursive analysts show their audience how they are using features of an extract in developing their claims about a piece of talk or text. That is, discursive analysts explicitly warrant their analytic claims by *demonstrating* their analysis in action. As demonstrated in Chapter 4, you can draw, for example, on features of grammar (pronouns, verb choices) and content (particular categories or concepts) used by speakers and writers to support your claims of the relevance of these features to their talk or text. In addition, you can support your analysis by showing how it is consistent with how "participants make visible their interpretations of each other's talk" (Wiggins, 2017, p. 136). For example, if a speaker treats another speaker's utterance as an insult, you can be justified in treating it this way as well. At all times, you will have to show the sequences of your analysis to capture the logic of the argument you are making (Wood & Kroger, 2000, p. 170) with regard both to a particular extract of talk or text and the patterns across extracts.

Of course, the versions of our analyses that we provide to our audiences through typical media such as conference presentations, journal articles, and book chapters tend to be ones that we have settled on (at least for the time being) and with which we are (reasonably) satisfied. They are more polished than the messy and circuitous fits and starts that constituted our analytic engagements with the data. Nevertheless, this explicit linking of claims to evidence, of taking your audience along with you as you analyze a piece of talk or text, is a hallmark of discursive analysis. How well you do this linking and showing will determine, in part, how convincing your analysis is for your audience and, in turn, their judgments about the quality of your work.

PLAUSIBILITY

Of course, demonstration must go hand-in-hand with *plausibility*. Your linking of analytic claims to evidence will be convincing to your audience to the extent that it is believable, or can be seen to be believable, to them. Here is where your knowledge of customs, norms, practices, and meanings that are specific to the context from which your data were derived comes into play in your interpretations of your data. Interpreting a discursive pattern in a way that is not believable by your audience is likely to undermine judgments of the quality of your work. In other words, the extent to which your audience shares the knowledge you rely on can determine whether and how your analysis resonates with them. However, even in instances where your analysis involves a novel discursive device or resource or where your analytic claims stretch into the unfamiliar, your work will be judged to be of higher quality if your audience can say, "I've never thought about 'X' before or in this way, but I can see how the analyst arrived at this interpretation, and it makes sense to me."

COHERENCE

Coherence captures the extent to which your analysis fits together and speaks to your research question(s). The inclusion and analysis of extracts of talk or text that do not appear, at face value, to be relevant to your research question(s) have the potential to result in judgments of poor quality by your readers. It is possible, of course, to mitigate this problem by acknowledging that an extract might appear, at first glance, to bear little relevance to your research question(s), but then to show explicitly in your analysis and interpretive claims how you are making a case for its relevance. Similarly, coherence in your analysis does not mean that the analysis of all extracts leads to the same analytic claims. Rather, your analysis has the potential to be judged as more rhetorically powerful and of higher quality if it shows how the nuances, inconsistencies, deviations, and even contradictions in the talk and text can be coherently accounted for by your claims. Seeking out negative cases or *counterinstances*—apparent contradictions between an instance of data and the claim you are making—and showing how they (a) can be accounted for by your analytic claims, (b) lead to a modified set of claims, or (c) fall outside the scope of your claims (Wood & Kroger, 2000, pp. 118–119) is another powerful way of demonstrating coherence. Wood and Kroger (2000) also included under this criterion "the requirement that a set of claims should . . . be characterized by a clear and adequate explanatory scope" (p. 174). That is, you should show how you are linking your claims to broader social contexts and how they have enabled you to meet the goals of your study (K. Tracy, 1995).

FRUITFULNESS

Fruitfulness captures the extent to which your analysis produces something considered to be of value by your readers. In the context of research, we often think of value in terms of newness—what novel ideas or insights have been produced. Sometimes, these new ways of understanding can be achieved by investigating a concept, practice, or discursive pattern that has previously not received attention. On other occasions, new ideas can come about by focusing on a well-researched topic in a different way—for example, by applying a discursive analytic perspective and set of practices to contemporary concerns such as climate change, immigration, and aging populations. Along with the other criteria outlined here, the quality of your study will be judged by the extent to which it engenders new ideas or questions for future investigations or fosters different ways of framing well-researched issues. In addition, the extent to which your work has implications for potentially productive social actions can be taken as an indicator of its value.

Although I have presented these criteria as separate from each other and in a separate chapter, I do so only to draw attention to their importance and not to suggest that they should be treated separately from the designing, conducting, and communicating of your study. Discursive analysts typically do not consider these criteria as a formal "check" on the quality of their work that requires explicitly reporting on them when communicating their research. Rather, how these criteria have been attended to is intimately woven into the analyst's decision-making processes and analytic practices involved in designing and conducting the research, and it is these processes and practices which, in turn, are made visible (to the extent possible) when the research is communicated. So, for example, although you do not have to include a separate section on these criteria when communicating your research, you do have to show (rather than tell) your audience that you have attended to them where it is fitting to do so.

7 ONGOING CONVERSATIONS

Over the years since the inception of discursive psychology, researchers who have embraced and critiqued this approach have shaped its contours and raised challenging ethical, conceptual, and methodological issues. In this final chapter, I briefly consider a few of these issues as a way of both alerting you to them and underscoring the vibrancy of discursive psychology.

QUESTIONS OF ETHICS

All research involving human participants is guided by a set of ethical principles, requirements, and practices. Although we typically associate these principles, requirements, and practices as being codified in documents produced by professional associations or societies (e.g., American Psychological Association, British Psychological Society, Canadian Psychological Association), they are, on occasion, incorporated into lists of criteria that can be used to judge the quality of qualitative research in general. An example of such a list is S. J. Tracy's (2010) eight "big tent" criteria for excellent qualitative research, which include, in addition to markers

https://doi.org/10.1037/0000220-007
Essentials of Discursive Psychology, by L. M. McMullen

of quality such as coherence and significant contribution covered in the previous chapter, procedural, situational, and relational ethics. However, as argued by Reicher (2000), the homogenizing of the diverse forms of qualitative inquiry under the general category of qualitative research and the application of a standardized set of criteria for judging quality across these diverse forms fails to consider the unique challenges encountered by discursive analysts.

Although conversations about questions of ethics that concern discursive analysts are ongoing, I outline three such questions to give you a sense of what is at stake.

What Constitutes Informed Consent in Interview-Based Discursive Studies?

In addition to informing interviewees about aspects of procedural ethics, such as that their participation is voluntary and can be ended at any point, that their data will be kept confidential, and what they can expect from participating in an interview, Hammersley (2014) raised the question of how far the notion of transparency extends. For example, does it extend to explaining to interviewees in interview-based discursive studies how their data will be analyzed? He argued that if researchers were to inform interviewees that the researchers are interested in the discursive practices they use, it is quite possible that the interviewees would not only feel deceived about the purpose of the interview but might also "become self-conscious about the language they use, perhaps editing it on the basis of some notion of 'good talk,' or at least trying to avoid 'bad talk'" (p. 532). In other words, according to Hammersley, being transparent about how the data will be analyzed could have the potential to expose deception and introduce even more reactivity in the data than otherwise occurs with the use of interviews in discursive studies. Apart from opting to use data in the public domain (which comes with its own set of ethical dilemmas), there is no easy solution to this issue. As Gorup (2019) concluded, "a certain level of deception" (p. 4) is perhaps inevitable in our use of this methodology in the context of data that are generated specifically for research purposes. In the end, you (perhaps in consultation with your supervisor or colleagues) will have to decide whether the potential significance and value of your research does or does not outweigh the risk of not soliciting fully informed consent from your participants. If you decide to proceed, you will have to deliberately consider how far you want to extend the notion of informed consent and for what purposes.

How Do Discursive Analysts Reconcile Their Close Scrutiny of People's Talk or Text in the Context of Using a Critical Mode of Interpretation With the Possibility That Our Interpretations Might Have Negative Effects?

Although in-depth dialogues on this question are needed, Wiggins (2017) provided what might be understood as a standard response to the concern about minimizing harm to participants in the context of discursive psychology:

> Remember that we are going to be analysing people's discursive practices, even if we never meet our participants directly, or seek to analyse them as individuals. We are going to be analysing their words in more detail than they might ever have imagined. So we need to be respectful of the fact that discourse is produced by people and that we may be delving into areas of their lives that could be private or very sensitive. Your research should never knowingly cause anyone harm, whether psychologically or physically, either at the time of data collection or *at the point of reporting and publishing research*. (p. 79, emphasis added)

As I have articulated elsewhere (McMullen, 2018), this statement reminds us of the importance of mitigating harm but does not unpack some of the dilemmas faced by discursive analysts. For example, I am still left with the following questions: If I can imagine the possibility that persons whose discursive practices I am analyzing will take my analysis as saying something about them as a person (even though this level of analysis is not the focus of discursive psychology) and possibly be negatively affected by it, how do I determine whether I should continue with or abandon this line of analysis? If I am critiquing a dominant culturally and temporally available discourse that I understand as being evident in a person's talk or text, how do I weigh the potential merit in foregrounding this discourse, showing ways in which it is constituted, and discussing its potential consequences against the possible harm that such a critique might produce should the person whose talk or text I am analyzing feel personally criticized by my analysis?

I have outlined possible ways to proceed: for example, aligning and readjusting, if necessary, conceptualizations of your relationships with participants with conceptualizations of the research process and being attuned to the risks and benefits of proceeding with particular sources of data and analytic foci (see McMullen, 2018, for more details). R. Josselson (personal communication, June 13, 2019) has also recommended a more direct approach—specifically, that at the end of interview-based research, we say to our interviewees, "I appreciate all you have shared with me, and I'm sure when I go to analyze this interview, I will learn a lot. But I want to tell you that what I am going to do with this material won't really be about *you*. Instead, I will be taking apart the text I transcribe and looking for language patterns for what they might say about larger social forces. . . . If you should read what I write, it will likely feel strange to you. But I want you to know, for now, that I am very, very grateful for your talking to me and helping me learn." Although I encourage you to consider such suggestions in consultation with your supervisor or colleagues, it is important to know that there are no easy answers to these questions.

What Ethical Issues Should You Consider When Using Online Data and Engaging in Internet-Mediated Research?

As discursive analysts have increasingly turned to the Internet as a source of data for their studies, questions about what constitutes ethical research practice have arisen. Such questions include, for example, "What counts as the public versus the private domain in online contexts?" "How should challenges to the anonymity (traceability) of data be handled?" "Under what circumstances should researchers identify themselves to those who manage or produce online data?" "When, from whom, and how should informed consent be solicited?" (e.g., Jowett, 2015, and Roberts, 2015). Although sets of guidelines on ethical practices in online research have been developed to assist researchers (e.g., the British Psychological Society, 2017), it is important to stress that, given the dynamic nature of technologies and how people use them, the landscape of what constitutes such practices is ever changing. In addition, much disagreement among researchers regarding what constitutes ethical practice in a particular online context still exists. You should not be surprised, then, to see divergences in how researchers respond to questions of ethics in the use of online data and internet-mediated research.

It is also possible that the nature of the research you are engaged in will require you to confront ethical questions that have not received much attention and demand a novel response. As Roberts (2015) articulated, even if you have weighed the risks and benefits of proceeding in a particular way at the outset of your online-based research project, you might be confronted with unanticipated ethical issues and dilemmas as you conduct your research. Although you have to be familiar with local, national, and international guidelines on conducting internet-based research, you should also prepare yourself for unexpected challenges. If such challenges arise, I recommend that you consult with your local institutional ethics board and/or colleagues and supervisors who can assist you in engaging in a process of reflexivity that is oriented to working through these challenges.

QUESTIONS RELATED TO CONCEPTUAL ADVANCEMENTS AND METHODOLOGICAL INNOVATIONS

Since the inception of the form of discursive research presented in this book, numerous debates regarding epistemology, methodology, boundaries, omissions, and the relation of this methodology to the discipline of psychology have transpired (e.g., Augoustinos & Tileagă, 2012). These debates continue and have led to questions that have crystallized some of the complexities and challenges in the way discursive psychology is conceptualized and used, including its relevance for investigations of so-called traditional domains of psychological focus, such as the individual person, affect, and experience. Here, I cite just three of the ways in which challenges to discursive psychology have been foregrounded and innovative methodological responses articulated.

To address the criticism that the person is absent or "vacated" in discursive research, Taylor (2015) proposed a way of theorizing a complex contemporary subject, which, she argued, can resolve some of the problems of conceptualizing a subject solely in discursive terms. Her account acknowledges that, although the subject is situated in particular contexts, it also has a unique and personal history that is built (and continues to be built) from resources (discursive and otherwise) that are given by situations and encounters and reused over time. In other words, a person brings to any situated encounter a constantly changing continuity. As part of this reconceptualization of the subject, Taylor proposed a research approach that combines, for example, a focus on personally specific narrative understandings of life experiences with a commitment to the notion that persons and whatever aspect of personhood is being investigated are socially constructed. According to Taylor, this dual commitment has the potential to hold together the unique aspects of the person's life history with its socially and culturally patterned discursive construction.

Similarly, as a way of more fully engaging with affect in discursive research, Wetherell (2013) theorized and demonstrated empirically how discourse and emotion are entangled and are mutually informed and informative when worked together. In focusing on the interwovenness of affective and discursive practices, Wetherell and colleagues (2019) used a variety of data-generating methods, including, for example, "walking alongside" and filming participants as they engage in an activity, focus groups, media analyses, and key informant interviews. Data that informed their analyses consisted of verbatim transcripts of discourse; detailed notes of, for example, facial expressions, gestures, and paralinguistic cues from the video recordings; and the researcher's and observer's readings of, for example, affect and context. From these diverse data, Wetherell and colleagues produced scenes of affective practices that interweave participants' expressions of affect with their discourse, alongside the researchers' readings of these expressions and meaning-making accounts.

Ways of addressing the longstanding critiques that discursive psychology deemphasizes broader social discourses (unlike critical discursive psychology) and ignores bodily experience in a phenomenological sense have also been proposed. To address the first critique, Cresswell (2012) sketched the broad contours of a methodological approach that combines the detailed focus of conversation analysis with notions from ethnomethodology, such as what can be learned by the breaching or breaking of social practices, as a way of articulating the broader social discourses on which people rely. Cresswell argued that attending to these breaches in conversation and the explanations and accounts that are put forward in response to such breaches can point "to 'theories-in-use' about taken-for-granted communal practices" (p. 558), including broader social discourses that are relied on but not necessarily made explicit by speakers and hearers. Similarly, in response to the second critique, he showed how the methodology of discursive psychology could be expanded by recognizing more fully that experience is accomplished in interaction. Doing so might involve, for example, paying closer attention to our own immediate bodily experiences as we engage with our research participants and/or our data and recognizing that we, as analysts, participate in an experience as we coconstruct and/or analyze and interpret our data.

FINAL THOUGHTS

I end with the unfinished conversations about ethical dilemmas, questions, and innovative developments related to discursive psychology to emphasize that all methodologies are dynamic. They are subject to revision, reconceptualization, and reinvention. They can also fall in and out of favor. To thrive, discursive psychology must continue to undergo changes and be met with challenges to how it is conceptualized and used. My brief presentation of it in this book is borne out of my engagement with this form of research and is a take that, I hope, will continue to be modified in creative and unexpected ways.

EXEMPLAR STUDIES

Edley, N., & Wetherell, M. (2001). Jekyll and Hyde: Men's constructions of feminism and feminists. *Feminism & Psychology, 11*(4), 439–457. https://doi.org/10.1177/0959353501011004002

Goodman, S., & Rowe, L. (2014). 'Maybe it is prejudice . . . but it is NOT racism': Negotiating racism in discussion forums about Gypsies. *Discourse & Society, 25*(1), 32–46. https://doi.org/10.1177/0957926513508856

Hanson-Easey, S., & Augoustinos, M. (2011). Complaining about humanitarian refugees: The role of sympathy talk in the design of complaints on talkback radio. *Discourse & Communication, 5*(3), 247–271. https://doi.org/10.1177/1750481311405588

Jowett, A. (2018). Gendered accounts of managing diabetes in same-sex relationships: A discursive analysis of partner support. *Health, 22*(2), 147–164. https://doi.org/10.1177/1363459316688518

Lafrance, M. N. (2011). Reproducing, resisting and transcending discourses of femininity: A discourse analysis of women's accounts of leisure. *Qualitative Research in Sport, Exercise and Health, 3*(1), 80–98. https://doi.org/10.1080/19398441.2010.541929

Locke, A., & Horton-Salway, M. (2010). 'Golden Age' versus 'Bad Old Days': A discursive examination of advice giving in antenatal classes. *Journal of Health Psychology, 15*(8), 1214–1224. https://doi.org/10.1177/1359105310364439

Marulanda, D., & Radtke, H. L. (2019). Men pursuing an undergraduate psychology degree: What's masculinity got to do with it? *Sex Roles, 81,* 338–354. https://doi.org/10.1007/s11199-018-0995-4

McMullen, L. M. (2012). Discourses of influence and autonomy in physicians' accounts of treatment decision making for depression. *Qualitative Health Research, 22*(2), 238–249. https://doi.org/10.1177/1049732311420738

McMullen, L. M. (2016). Decoupling antidepressants and depression in accounts of being prescribed antidepressants off-label. *Qualitative Psychology, 3*(2), 145–158. https://doi.org/10.1037/qup0000038

McVittie, C., McKinlay, A., & Widdicombe, S. (2008). Organizational knowledge and discourse of diversity in employment. *Journal of Organizational Change Management, 21*(3), 348–366. https://doi.org/10.1108/09534810810874822

Tileagă, C. (2011). (Re) writing biography: Memory, identity, and textually mediated reality in coming to terms with the past. *Culture and Psychology, 17*(2), 197–215. https://doi.org/10.1177/1354067X11398315

Versteeg, W., te Molder, H., & Sneijder, P. (2018). "Listen to your body": Participants' alternative to science in online health discussions. *Health, 22*(5), 432–450. https://doi.org/10.1177/1363459317695632

Wiggins, S. (2014). On the accountability of changing bodies: Using discursive psychology to examine embodied identities in different research settings. *Qualitative Psychology, 1*(2), 144. https://doi.org/10.1037/qup0000012

Appendix B

COMMONLY USED TRANSCRIPTION NOTATIONS

(.)	short, untimed pause
(2)	timed pause in seconds
<u>only</u>	emphasis through volume and/or pitch
↑	onset of rising pitch
↓	onset of descending pitch
>you know<	talk noticeably quicker than surrounding talk
°cover it up°	talk noticeably quieter than surrounding talk
nee:d	stretching out of preceding sound
[mhm] [upset]	overlapping talk
(.hh)	audible inhalation
i-	sharp cut-off of word
. . .	line of text omitted

EXAMPLES OF DISCURSIVE DEVICES AND RESOURCES

Argument types: use of syllogisms; offering reasons, explanations, or justifications for a claim; offensive rhetoric (the undermining of alternatives); defensive rhetoric (having the capacity to resist discounting or undermining)

Categories: classifications of various sorts, such as membership (e.g., mother, Irish, activist), emotions (e.g., accounts of actions as expressions of feelings), cognitions (e.g., accounts of actions as expressions of thoughts, opinions, beliefs, attitudes) that are used to accomplish a range of social actions

Category entitlements: what follows from particular categories—the sorts of privileges, responsibilities, knowledge, skills, expectations, and so forth to which a category (e.g., working mother, expert) is entitled

Consensus and corroboration: reporting something as if others agree (consensus) or as if it is independently supported by others (corroboration) can be used to construct or enhance the facticity of an account

Details versus vagueness: use of vivid details to construct a credible account of events or being systematically vague—producing an account that is lacking in clarity—to inoculate oneself against charges of being too invested in a particular account

Disclaimers: short phrases, such as "I'm not against immigration, but . . . ," used to mitigate one's stance on a particular issue

Extreme case formulations: words or phrases that are both semantically extreme and oriented to as extreme

Footing: often exemplified by shifts in pronoun use; indicates the position or role from which one is speaking (e.g., saying one's own words, speaking as if relaying someone else's words, or speaking as the person responsible for the talk); used to identify accountability

Hedging: use of conditionals (e.g., "might," "would," "could"), modifiers (e.g., "probably"), indefinite articles (e.g., "a") to mark a statement as provisional and suggest there are alternatives to the claim being made

Interpretative repertoires: conceptually organized clusters of terms, phrases, grammatical features, figures of speech that are used to construct versions of events, practices, actions, persons, and so forth, and to perform a variety of actions

Lists and contrasts: listing of items in a sequence can be used to enhance the completeness of an account and/or, particularly in the case of a three-part list (Jefferson, 1990), to signal a completion point; contrasts or comparisons are used to emphasize one thing over another as a way of bolstering a claim

Management of stake or interest: a range of practices used by speakers or writers to prevent one's talk or writing from being undermined, specifically via charges that one has a stake or interest in what one is saying or writing; or, conversely, to discount the truth of a claim made by another person by referencing their stake or interest in what they are saying or writing

Markers: words or phrases that do not contribute to propositional meaning (e.g., "like," "well," "however") but can serve a variety of social functions; *concessionary markers* include words or phrases such as "okay," "of course," "you know," "fair enough," which indicate that a speaker or writer is agreeing to a position on which they have previously disagreed; *contrastive conjunction markers* include words or phrases such as "but," "nevertheless," "anyway," which signal that the concessionary material is finished and that what comes next is in opposition to what has been said previously

Minimization: use of words such as "just," "only," "a little bit" to treat the extent of something as insignificant or less serious

Modal expressions: words (e.g., "probably") and phrases (e.g., "I think," "I guess," "I could") used to indicate the speaker's degree of ability, obligation, intention, or permission to be able to perform that activity

Narratives: construction of stories or anecdotes for a particular rhetorical effect

Personal pronouns: words such as "we," "I," "they" used to construct relations of status and/or solidarity

Positioning: the constitution of speakers and hearers in particular ways; for example, the agent–patient distinction refers to whether the speaker or the person spoken about is constructed as actively making choices and determining the course of behavior or as suffering the consequences of other forces; a way of managing accountability for actions

Reported speech: presenting a position by attributing it to others, either through *direct speech* (i.e., as a reproduction or quotation of the [exact] words initially uttered by another speaker in a different context) or *indirect speech* (i.e., as a summary or paraphrase of speech uttered by another speaker)

Silences, pauses, and hesitations: breaks or gaps in the flow of speaking or writing that can serve a variety of functions

Tropes: figures of speech, such as metaphors, similes, and analogies that can be used to make a comparison or produce a particular rhetorical effect

References

Abell, J., & Stokoe, E. H. (2001). Broadcasting the royal role: Constructing culturally situated identities in the Princess Diana *Panorama* interview. *British Journal of Social Psychology*, *40*(3), 417–435. https://doi.org/10.1348/014466601164902

Alasuutari, M., & Järvi, A. (2012). "My dad got depression, or something": How do children talk about parental mental disorder? *Qualitative Research in Psychology*, *9*(2), 134–150. https://doi.org/10.1080/14780880903414250

Alexander, E., & McMullen, L. M. (2015). Constructions of motherhood and fatherhood in newspaper articles on maternal and paternal postpartum depression. *Gender and Language*, *9*(2), 143–166. https://doi.org/10.1558/genl.v9i2.17318

American Psychiatric Association. (2013). *Diagnostic and statistical manual of mental disorders* (5th ed.). https://doi.org/10.1176/appi.books.9780890425596

American Psychological Association. (2020). *Publication manual of the American Psychological Association* (7th ed.). https://doi.org/10.1037/0000165-000

Antaki, C., Billig, M. G., Edwards, D., & Potter, J. A. (2003). Discourse analysis means doing analysis: A critique of six analytic shortcomings. *Discourse Analysis Online, 1*. https://extra.shu.ac.uk/daol/articles/open/2002/002/antaki2002002-paper.html

Antaki, C., & Widdicombe, S. (1998). Identity as an achievement and as a tool. In C. Antaki & S. Widdicombe (Eds.), *Identities in talk* (pp. 1–14). SAGE.

Augoustinos, M., & Tileagă, C. (2012). Twenty five years of discursive psychology. *British Journal of Social Psychology*, *51*(3), 405–412. https://doi.org/10.1111/j.2044-8309.2012.02096.x

Austin, J. (1962). *How to do things with words*. Clarendon Press.

Babineau, C., McMullen, L., & Downe, P. (2017). Negotiating what constitutes depression: Focus group conversations in response to viewing direct-to-consumer advertisements for antidepressants. *Canadian Journal of Communication*, *42*(5), 725–743. https://doi.org/10.22230/cjc.2017v4n5a3175

Baker, S. E., & Edwards, R. (2012). *How many qualitative interviews is enough? Expert voices and early career reflections on sampling and cases in qualitative research*. National Centre for Research Methods.

Barbour, R. (2018). *Doing focus groups* (2nd ed.). SAGE.

Bowleg, L., Heckert, A. L., Brown, T. L., & Massie, J. S. (2015). Responsible men, blameworthy women: Black heterosexual men's discursive constructions of safer sex and masculinity. *Health Psychology, 34*(4), 314–327. https://doi.org/10.1037/hea0000216

British Psychological Society. (2017). *Ethics guidelines for Internet-mediated research*. https://www.bps.org.uk/news-and-policy/ethics-guidelines-internet-mediated-research-2017

Burr, V. (1995). *An introduction to social constructionism*. Routledge. https://doi.org/10.4324/9780203133026

Chamberlain, K., McGuigan, K., Anstiss, D., & Marshall, K. (2018). A change of view: Arts-based research and psychology. *Qualitative Research in Psychology, 15*(2–3), 131–139. https://doi.org/10.1080/14780887.2018.1456590

Coates, L., & Wade, A. (2007). Language and violence: Analysis of four discursive operations. *Journal of Family Violence, 22*(7), 511–522. https://doi.org/10.1007/s10896-007-9082-2

Cresswell, J. (2012). Including social discourses and experience in research on refugees, race, and ethnicity. *Discourse & Society, 23*(5), 553–575. https://doi.org/10.1177/0957926512455885

Crotty, M. (1998). *The foundations of social research: Meaning and perspective in the research process*. SAGE.

Davies, B., & Harré, R. (1990). Positioning: The discursive production of selves. *Journal for the Theory of Social Behaviour, 20*(1), 43–63. https://doi.org/10.1111/j.1468-5914.1990.tb00174.x

Edley, N., & Wetherell, M. (2001). Jekyll and Hyde: Men's constructions of feminism and feminists. *Feminism & Psychology, 11*(4), 439–457. https://doi.org/10.1177/0959353501011004002

Edwards, D. (2005). Moaning, whinging and laughing: The subjective side of complaints. *Discourse Studies, 7*(1), 5–29. https://doi.org/10.1177/1461445605048765

Edwards, D., & Potter, J. (1992). *Discursive psychology*. SAGE.

Elliott, R., Fischer, C. T., & Rennie, D. L. (1999). Evolving guidelines for publication of qualitative research studies in psychology and related fields. *British Journal of Clinical Psychology, 38*(3), 215–229. https://doi.org/10.1348/014466599162782

Every, D., & Augoustinos, M. (2007). Constructions of racism in the Australian parliamentary debates on asylum seekers. *Discourse & Society, 18*(4), 411–436. https://doi.org/10.1177/0957926507077427

Gergen, K. J., & Gergen, M. M. (2018). Doing things with words: Toward evocative ethnography. *Qualitative Research in Psychology, 15*(2–3), 272–286. https://doi.org/10.1080/14780887.2018.1430004

Goodman, S., & Burke, S. (2010). 'Oh you don't want asylum seekers, oh you're just racist': A discursive analysis of discussions about whether it's racist to oppose asylum seeking. *Discourse & Society, 21*(3), 325–340. https://doi.org/10.1177/0957926509360743

Gorup, M. (2019). Ethics of discourse analysis. In R. Iphofen (Ed.), *Handbook of research ethics and scientific integrity* (pp. 1–22). Springer Nature. https://doi.org/10.1007/978-3-319-76040-7_22-1

Hammersley, M. (2014). On the ethics of interviewing for discourse analysis. *Qualitative Research, 14*(5), 529–541. https://doi.org/10.1177/1468794113495039

Harper, D. J. (1994). The professional construction of 'paranoia' and the discursive use of diagnostic criteria. *The British Journal of Medical Psychology, 67*(2), 131–143. https://doi.org/10.1111/j.2044-8341.1994.tb01779.x

Horne, J., & Wiggins, S. (2009). Doing being 'on the edge': Managing the dilemma of being authentically suicidal in an online forum. *Sociology of Health & Illness, 31*(2), 170–184. https://doi.org/10.1111/j.1467-9566.2008.01130.x

Jefferson, G. (1990). List construction as a task and resource. In G. Psathas (Ed.), *Interaction competence: Studies in ethnomethodology and conversation analysis* (pp. 63–92). University Press of America.

Jefferson, G. (2004). Glossary of transcript symbols with an introduction. In G. H. Lerner (Ed.), *Conversation analysis: Studies from the first generation* (pp. 13–31). John Benjamins. https://doi.org/10.1075/pbns.125.02jef

Josselson, R. (2013). *Interviewing for qualitative inquiry: A relational approach.* Guilford Press.

Jowett, A. (2015). A case for using online discussion forums in critical psychological research. *Qualitative Research in Psychology, 12*(3), 287–297. https://doi.org/10.1080/14780887.2015.1008906

Kurz, T., Augoustinos, M., & Crabb, S. (2010). Contesting the 'national interest' and maintaining 'our lifestyle': A discursive analysis of political rhetoric around climate change. *British Journal of Social Psychology, 49*(3), 601–625. https://doi.org/10.1348/014466609X481173

Kurz, T., Donaghue, N., Rapley, M., & Walker, I. (2005). The ways that people talk about natural resources: Discursive strategies as barriers to environmentally sustainable practices. *British Journal of Social Psychology, 44*(4), 603–620. https://doi.org/10.1348/014466604X18064

Ladd-Taylor, M., & Umansky, L. (Eds.). (1998). *"Bad" mothers: The politics of blame in twentieth-century America.* NYU Press.

Lawes, R. (1999). Marriage: An analysis of discourse. *British Journal of Social Psychology, 38*(1), 1–20. https://doi.org/10.1348/014466699164004

Lawless, M., Augoustinos, M., & LeCouteur, A. (2018). "Your brain matters": Issues of risk and responsibility in online dementia prevention information. *Qualitative Health Research, 28*(10), 1539–1551. https://doi.org/10.1177/1049732317732962

Levitt, H. M., Bamberg, M., Creswell, J. W., Frost, D. M., Josselson, R., & Suárez-Orozco, C. (2018). Journal article reporting standards for qualitative primary, qualitative meta-analytic, and mixed methods research in psychology: The APA Publications and Communications Board task force report. *American Psychologist, 73*(1), 26–46. https://doi.org/10.1037/amp0000151

Levitt, H. M., Motulsky, S. L., Wertz, F. J., Morrow, S. L., & Ponterotto, J. G. (2017). Recommendations for designing and reviewing qualitative research in psychology: Promoting methodological integrity. *Qualitative Psychology, 4*(1), 2–22. https://doi.org/10.1037/qup0000082

Lofgren, A., Hewitt, V., & das Nair, R. (2015). Doing fence sitting: A discursive analysis of clinical psychologists' constructions of mental health. *Qualitative Health Research, 25*(4), 470–485. https://doi.org/10.1177/1049732314549479

Magnusson, E., & Marecek, J. (2015). *Doing interview-based qualitative research: A learner's guide.* Cambridge University Press. https://doi.org/10.1017/CBO9781107449893

McMullen, L. M. (1999). Metaphors in the talk of 'depressed' women in psychotherapy. *Canadian Psychology, 40*(2), 102–111. https://doi.org/10.1037/h0086830

McMullen, L. M. (2003). "Depressed" women's constructions of the deficient self. In J. M. Stoppard & L. M. McMullen (Eds.), *Situating sadness: Women and depression in social context* (pp. 17–38). New York University Press.

McMullen, L. M. (2005). Talk about receiving, giving, and taking in radio interviews: 'Doing modesty' and 'making a virtue out of necessity'. *British Journal of Social Psychology, 44*(4), 557–570. https://doi.org/10.1348/014466604X18532

McMullen, L. M. (2008). Fact sheets as gendered narratives of depression. In H. Clark (Ed.), *Depression and narrative: Telling the dark* (pp. 127–142). State University of New York Press.

McMullen, L. M. (2011). A discursive analysis of Teresa's protocol: Enhancing oneself, diminishing others. In F. J. Wertz, K. Charmaz, L. M. McMullen, R. Josselson, R. Anderson, & E. McSpadden, *Five ways of doing qualitative analysis: Phenomenological psychology, grounded theory, discourse analysis, narrative research, and intuitive inquiry* (pp. 205–223). Guilford Press.

McMullen, L. M. (2012). Discourses of influence and autonomy in physicians' accounts of treatment decision making for depression. *Qualitative Health Research, 22*(2), 238–249. https://doi.org/10.1177/1049732311420738

McMullen, L. M. (2016). Decoupling antidepressants and depression in accounts of being prescribed antidepressants off-label. *Qualitative Psychology, 3*(2), 145–158. https://doi.org/10.1037/qup0000038

McMullen, L. M. (2018). Critical discursive psychology and relational ethics: An uneasy tension? *Social and Personality Psychology Compass, 12*(11), e12420. https://doi.org/10.1111/spc3.12420

McMullen, L. M., & Conway, J. B. (2002). Conventional metaphors for depression. In S. R. Fussell (Ed.), *The verbal communication of emotions: Interdisciplinary perspectives* (pp. 167–181). Erlbaum.

McMullen, L. M., & Herman, J. (2009). Women's accounts of their decision to quit taking antidepressants. *Qualitative Health Research, 19*(11), 1569–1579. https://doi.org/10.1177/1049732309349936

McMullen, L. M., & Sigurdson, K. J. (2014). Depression is to diabetes as antidepressants are to insulin: The unraveling of an analogy? *Health Communication, 29*(3), 309–317. https://doi.org/10.1080/10410236.2012.753660

McMullen, L. M., & Stoppard, J. M. (2006). Women and depression: A case study of the influence of feminism in Canadian psychology. *Feminism & Psychology, 16*(3), 273–288. https://doi.org/10.1177/0959353506067847

McNeill, A., Lyons, E., & Pehrson, S. (2014). Reconstructing apology: David Cameron's Bloody Sunday apology in the press. *British Journal of Social Psychology, 53*(4), 656–674. https://doi.org/10.1111/bjso.12053

Parker, I. (2005). *Qualitative psychology: Introducing radical research*. Open University Press.

Paulson, J. F., & Bazemore, S. D. (2010). Prenatal and postpartum depression in fathers and its association with maternal depression: A meta-analysis. *JAMA, 303*(19), 1961–1969. https://doi.org/10.1001/jama.2010.605

Potter, J. (1998). Discursive social psychology: From attitudes to evaluative practices. *European Review of Social Psychology, 9*(1), 233–266. https://doi.org/10.1080/14792779843000090

Potter, J. (2003). Discourse analysis and discursive psychology. In P. M. Camic, J. E. Rhodes, & L. Yardley (Eds.), *Qualitative research in psychology: Expanding perspectives in methodology and design* (pp. 73–94). American Psychological Association. https://doi.org/10.1037/10595-005

Potter, J. (2012). Discourse analysis and discursive psychology. In H. Cooper, P. M. Camic, D. L. Long, A. T. Panter, D. Rindskopf, & K. J. Sher (Eds.), *APA handbook of research methods in psychology: Vol. 2. Research designs: Quantitative, qualitative, neuropsychological, and biological* (pp. 119–138). American Psychological Association. https://doi.org/10.1037/13620-008

Potter, J., & Hepburn, A. (2005). Qualitative interviews in psychology: Problems and possibilities. *Qualitative Research in Psychology, 2*(4), 281–307. https://doi.org/10.1191/1478088705qp045oa

Potter, J., & Wetherell, M. (1987). *Discourse and social psychology*. SAGE.

Puchta, C., & Potter, J. (2004). *Focus group practice*. SAGE. https://doi.org/10.4135/9781849209168

Reicher, S. (2000). Against methodolatry: Some comments on Elliott, Fischer, and Rennie. *British Journal of Clinical Psychology, 39*(1), 1–6. https://doi.org/10.1348/014466500163031

Roberts, L. D. (2015). Ethical issues in conducting qualitative research in online communities. *Qualitative Research in Psychology, 12*(3), 314–325. https://doi.org/10.1080/14780887.2015.1008909

Sakki, I., & Pettersson, K. (2016). Discursive constructions of otherness in populist radical right political blogs. *European Journal of Social Psychology, 46*(2), 156–170. https://doi.org/10.1002/ejsp.2142

Sigurdson, K. J., & McMullen, L. M. (2013). Talking controversy: Long-term users of antidepressants and the diagnosis of depression. *Qualitative Research in Psychology*, *10*(4), 428–444. https://doi.org/10.1080/14780887.2011.647260

Silverman, D. (2017). How was it for you? The Interview Society and the irresistible rise of the (poorly analyzed) interview. *Qualitative Research*, *17*(2), 144–158. https://doi.org/10.1177/1468794116668231

Smaling, A. (2003). Inductive, analogical, and communicative generalization. *International Journal of Qualitative Methods*, 52–67. http://dx.doi.org/10.1177/160940690300200105

Stiles, W. (1993). Quality control in qualitative research. *Clinical Psychology Review*, *13*(6), 593–618. https://doi.org/10.1016/0272-7358(93)90048-Q

Stoppard, J. M., & McMullen, L. M. (Eds.). (2003). *Situating sadness: Women and depression in social context*. New York University Press.

Tagliamonte, S. (2005). So who? Like how? Just what?: Discourse markers in the conversations of young Canadians. *Journal of Pragmatics*, *37*(11), 1896–1915. https://doi.org/10.1016/j.pragma.2005.02.017

Taylor, S. (2015). Discursive and psychosocial? Theorising a complex contemporary subject. *Qualitative Research in Psychology*, *12*(1), 8–21. https://doi.org/10.1080/14780887.2014.958340

Tracy, K. (1995). Action-implicative discourse analysis. *Journal of Language and Social Psychology*, *14*(1–2), 195–215. https://doi.org/10.1177/0261927X95141011

Tracy, S. J. (2010). Qualitative quality: Eight "big tent" criteria for excellent qualitative research. *Qualitative Inquiry*, *16*(10), 837–851. https://doi.org/10.1177/1077800410383121

Valiakalayil, A. (2015). *Stress and depression discourses on self-help websites: What is their relation in the online context?* [Doctoral dissertation, University of Saskatchewan]. University of Saskatchewan HARVEST. https://harvest.usask.ca/handle/10388/ETD-2015-09-2262

Wallwork, J., & Dixon, J. A. (2004). Foxes, green fields and Britishness: On the rhetorical construction of place and national identity. *British Journal of Social Psychology*, *43*(1), 21–39. https://doi.org/10.1348/014466604322915962

Wetherell, M. (1998). Positioning and interpretative repertoires: Conversation analysis and post-structuralism in dialogue. *Discourse & Society*, *9*(3), 387–412. https://doi.org/10.1177/0957926598009003005

Wetherell, M. (2013). Affect and discourse—What's the problem? From affect as excess to affective/discursive practice. *Subjectivity*, *6*(4), 349–368. https://doi.org/10.1057/sub.2013.13

Wetherell, M., McConville, A., & McCreanor, T. (2019). Defrosting the freezer and other acts of quiet resistance: Affective practice theory, everyday activism and affective dilemmas. *Qualitative Research in Psychology*, *17*(1), 1–23. http://dx.doi.org/10.1080/14780887.2019.1581310

Wetherell, M., & Potter, J. (1993). *Mapping the language of racism: Discourse and the legitimation of exploitation*. Columbia University Press.

Whitehead, K., & Kurz, T. (2008). Saints, sinners and standards of femininity: Discursive constructions of anorexia nervosa and obesity in women's magazines. *Journal of Gender Studies*, *17*(4), 345–358. https://doi.org/10.1080/09589230802420086

Wiggins, S. (2017). *Discursive psychology: Theory, method and applications.* SAGE. https://doi.org/10.4135/9781473983335

Williams, K., Kurz, T., Summers, M., & Crabb, S. (2013). Discursive constructions of infant feeding: The dilemma of mothers' 'guilt'. *Feminism & Psychology*, *23*(3), 339–358. https://doi.org/10.1177/0959353512444426

Willig, C. (2001). *Introducing qualitative research in psychology: Adventures in theory and method.* Open University Press.

Wood, L. A., & Kroger, R. O. (2000). *Doing discourse analysis: Methods for studying action in talk and text.* SAGE.

Wood, L. A., & Rennie, H. (1994). Formulating rape: The discursive construction of victims and villains. *Discourse & Society*, *5*(1), 125–148. https://doi.org/10.1177/0957926594005001006

Index

A

Abell, J., 22–23
Absences, in data, 36–37
Abstract, article, 68–69
Accounts, 12, 71
Action orientation, 10–11
Affect, 83–84
Alasuutari, M., 18–19
Alexander, E., 46–55
American Psychological Association (APA), 68
Analogical generalizability, 70
Analogy, detailed analysis related to, 40–46
Analysis section, of article, 69
Analytic claims. *See* Claims, analytic
Anecdotes, 36
Antaki, C., 40
APA (American Psychological Association), 68
Archival documents
    data collection from, 28–29
    as data source, 22–23
    and ethics approval, 27
Arguments
    about meaning and significance, 54
    structure of, 44–45
    types of, 89
Arts-based dissemination approaches, 72
ATLAS.ti, 36
Austin, J., 10

B

Babineau, Christine, 25, 32
Backgrounding, 52
Bashir, Martin, 22

Bazemore, S. D., 46
"Big tent" criteria, 79–80
Bodily experience, 84
Books and book chapters, dissemination in, 72
Bowleg, L., 68
Burke, S., 19
Burr, V., 7–8

C

Canadian Psychological Association (CPA), 28
Canadian Psychology, 72
Categories, 89
Causality statements, 71
Claims, analytic
    in analysis of social action, 60
    assessing, with research team, 64
    coherence of, 76
    demonstrating support for, 74–75
    in detailed analyses of extracts, 39, 42–43
    in discursive psychology, 13
    plausibility of, 75
Clusters, of data, 38–39
Coates, L., 55–56
Cognition, talk as route to, 9
Cognitivism, 4
Coherence, 76
Collaboration, on data analysis, 63–64
Comparative analytic stance, 52–54
Comparisons, 90
Concept construction, 46–55

Concessionary markers, 90
Conference presentations, 72
Consensus, 64, 89
Consent, informed, 80
Constructionism
    consensus on analysis in, 64
    defined, 7
    in discursive psychology, 7–8
    writing manuscripts consistent with,
        70–72
Consultations, 64
Context
    for analysis of social actions, 55
    in critical discursive psychology, 5–6
    cultural, 12, 50–51
    for data extracts, 47–49
    in discursive psychology, 8, 12
    and plausibility of claims, 75
    for research questions, 19–20
    situating discourse in, 11
    social, 9–10, 12
Contrastive conjunction markers, 90
Contrasts, 90
Conversation analysis, 4, 5, 32–33
Corroboration, 89
Counterinstances, 76
CPA (Canadian Psychological Association),
    28
Cresswell, J., 84
Critical discourse analysis, 4
Critical discursive psychology, 5–6
Critical theory, 8
Crotty, M., 3, 7, 8
Cultural context
    in analysis of concept construction, 50–51
    in discursive psychology, 12
Cultural practices, discursive research on,
    46

D

Data, structural features of, 51–52
Data analysis, 35–65
    additional data collection after, 29
    for concept construction, 46–55
    concluding process of, 64–65
    on device employment and effects,
        40–46
    engaging others in, 63–64
    examples of detailed analyses, 40–64
    framing research question during, 20
    grouping data extracts for, 38–39

    making notes in, 36–37
    process of, 35–40
    reading/listening to data set in, 35–36
    selecting data extracts for, 37–38
    selecting extracts for detailed analysis,
        39–40
    on social action performance, 55–63
Data collection
    from archival documents, 28–29
    concluding, 29
    and research design, 22
    selection criteria for, 22–23
    use of term, 71
Data extracts
    coherence in inclusion of, 76
    demonstrating analysis of, 74–75
    for detailed analysis, 39–40
    drawing on text/talk outside of, 63
    grouping, 38–39
    line numbers for, 33
    in manuscripts, 70
    and research question, 37–38
    selecting, 37–40
Data generation
    electing to use new data, 23–25
    ethics approval for, 27
    from interviews or focus groups, 29–33
    notational detail for, 32–33
    recording and transcribing information
        in, 32
    and research design, 22
    research participant selection and
        recruitment for, 23–25
    use of term, 71
Data selection
    criteria for, 22–23
    use of term, 71
Data set
    number of interviews in, 31
    reading or listening to entire, 35–36
    structure of, 52
Data sources
    archival documents, 22–23
    and framing of research question, 20–21
    for new data, 23–25
    selecting, 21–25
Data units, 28
Defensive rhetoric, 89
Demonstration, 74–75
Details, vagueness vs., 89
Diana, Princess of Wales, 22
Direct speech, 91

Disclaimers, 89
Discourse
  action orientation of, 10
  defined, 4
  and emotion, 83
  sequential organization of, 11
  social, 84
Discourse analysis
  analyst's influence on, 12
  critical, 4
  defined, 4
  everyday activities vs., 3
  Foucauldian, 4
  journals specializing in, 67–68
"Discovery," use of term, 71
Discursive devices, 89–91
  analyzing context for, 45–46
  analyzing employment/effects of, 40–46
  familiarization with, 37
  interpreting functions of, 45
Discursive psychology
  challenges with, 7
  choosing, 6–10
  cognitivism vs., 9–10
  context in, 12
  critical, 5–6
  deciding to use, 13–14
  defined, 5, 6
  epistemology, 7–8
  ethical issues with, 79–82
  evidence, claims, and interpretations
    in, 13
  focus of, 10
  future of, 84
  goal of, 9
  knowledge production process in, 8–9
  language use in, 10–12
  methodological innovations addressing
    criticisms of, 83–84
  theoretical perspective of, 8
  versions and accounts in, 12
Discursive research, 72–77. *See also*
    Research dissemination
  affect in, 83–84
  best practices for, 73
  bodily experience in, 84
  coherence of, 76
  demonstration in, 74–75
  documentation for, 74
  fruitfulness of, 76–77
  journals devoted to, 16
  plausibility of, 75

reconceptualization of subject in, 83
  social discourse in, 84
Discursive social psychology, 5
Discussion section, of article, 69
Dissemination of research. *See* Research
    dissemination
Documentation, 23, 28, 74
"Doing," in analysis of social action, 56

E

Elliott, R., 73
"Emergence," use of term, 71
Emotion, discourse and, 83–84
Emphasis, 45
Entitlements, category, 89
Ethical issues, 27, 79–82
Ethnomethodology, 84
Everyday practices, discursive analysis
    of, 19
Evidence
    in analysis of social action, 59
    in discursive psychology, 13
    linking of claims to, 74–75
    providing, 39
Exemplar studies, 85–86
Experimental research, 8
Extreme case formulations, 89

F

"Factors," use of term, 71
Fact sheets, selecting, 28
Figures of speech, 19, 45
"Findings," use of term, 70–71
Focus groups, 31–33
Footing, 90
Foregrounding, 52
Foucauldian discourse analysis, 4
Fruitfulness, 76–77

G

Generalizability, 70, 72
Goodman, S., 19
Gorup, M., 80
Gray literature, 16

H

Hammersley, M., 80
Harm, minimizing, 81–82

Health-related topics, research on, 46
Hedging, 90
Herman, J., 18
Hesitation, 91
Horne, J., 56
"How" research questions, 9, 17–19
Hyperbole, 48
Hypothetico-deductive method, 8

I

Identity positions, 19
Ideologies, research on, 46
Inclusion criteria
    for data extracts, 39–40
    for research participants, 23–24
Indirect speech, 91
Individual person, in discursive
        psychology, 10, 83
Informed consent, 80
Interest, management of, 90
Interpretations
    in analysis of social action, 59, 63
    assessing, with research team, 64
    causality statements about, 71
    in detailed analyses of extracts, 51
    in discursive psychology, 13
    negative effects of, for participants, 81–82
Interpretative repertoires, 5, 90
Interviewee, 29, 30, 81
Interviewer, 29, 30, 60, 81
Interviews, research. *See* Research
        interviews
Introduction, article, 69
Iteration
    in data analysis, 39, 41, 47
    in study design, 17, 21

J

Järvi, A., 18–19
Jefferson, G., 32
Jefferson lite approach, 33, 87
Josselson, R., 81–82
Journal Article Reporting Standards for
        Qualitative Research (Levitt et al.),
        68
Journals
    article structure in, 68–70
    preparing manuscripts for publication
        in, 67–72
Justice issues, discursive research on, 46

K

Key words lists, identifying extracts with,
    47
Kijiji.ca, 25
Kroger, R. O., 36, 37, 58, 74, 76
Kurz, T., 18, 20

L

Language use
    in discursive psychology, 10–12
    in manuscripts, 70–72
Lawless, M., 20
Levitt, H. M., 68, 73
Line numbers, transcript, 33
Linguistic devices, 6–7. *See also* Discursive
    devices
Linguistics, 4
Listening, to full corpus of data, 35–36
Listing, 90
Literature review, 69
Literature search, initial, 16–17
Lofgren, A., 56

M

Manuscripts
    preparing, for publication, 67–72
    writing, 70–72
Markers, 90
MAXQDA, 36
McMullen, L. M., 18, 21, 24, 28, 30–31,
    40–58, 72
Meaning, arguments about, 54
Methodology and Methods section,
    of article, 69
Micro features, of interaction, 5
Minimization, 90
Modal expression words and phrases, 42,
    90
Moderator, focus group, 31

N

Narratives, 36, 70, 90
Newness, fruitfulness as, 76–77
Non-content related features, 49–50
Nonlexical sounds, 11
Notational detail, level of, 32–33
Notations, transcription, 32, 87
Note taking, 36–37
NVivo, 36

O

Objectivism, 7, 70–71
Obvious, stating the, 29, 36, 58
Offensive rhetoric, 89
Online data sources
    collecting data from, 28–29
    ethical issues with, 82
    selecting, 21
Opening topic statement, 15–16

P

Paralinguistic features, 10, 11, 45, 63
Parallelism, 50
Paulson, J. F., 46
Pauses, 91
Person, in discursive psychology, 10, 83
Personal pronouns, 90
Plausibility, 75
Political issues, discursive research on, 46
Positioning, 91
Postpositivism, 8
Potter, J., 5, 6, 10, 12
Presentations, research, 72
Presupposing, 47
Pronouns, personal, 90
Psychological concepts, 5
Psychological constructs, in manuscripts, 71
Publication, 67–72
Publication Manual of the American
    Psychological Association, 68

Q

Qualifiers, 44
Qualitative research
    assessing quality of, 73
    "big tent" criteria for, 79–80
    journals devoted to, 16

R

Reactions, to data, 36, 50
Readings
    of data extracts, 38–39
    of full corpus of data, 35–36
Realism, 8, 71
Recordings, securing, 32
Recruitment, research participant, 24–25
Reflexivity, 16
Reicher, S., 80
Reliability, 73, 74

Reported speech, 44, 91
Research dissemination, 67–72
    addressing quality criteria during, 77
    innovative forms of, 67, 72
    journal article structure, 68–70
    preparing manuscripts for publication,
        67–72
    writing manuscripts, 70–72
Research interviews
    criticism of, 29–30
    data generation in, 22, 29–31
    informed consent for, 80
    minimizing harm for participants in,
        81–82
    number of, in data set, 31
    protocols for, 30–31
Research participants
    informed consent from, 80
    minimizing harm to, 81–82
    selection and recruitment of, 23–25
Research question(s)
    changing, 17
    for discursive psychology, 6–9
    framing, 17–21
    "how" questions, 9, 17–19
    and methodology, 13
    selecting data extracts that speak to,
        37–38
    "what" questions, 9, 17–19
    "why" questions, 9, 19
Research teams, data analysis by, 63–64
Rhetoric, offensive and defensive, 89
Roberts, L. D., 82

S

Sample size, 72
Sarcasm, 48
Sensory data, 21
Sequential organization, of discourse, 11
Significance, arguments about, 54
Sigurdson, K. J., 40–46
Silences, 91
Social action(s)
    analyzing data on, 55–63
    discursive analysis of, 19
    in discursive psychology, 5, 10–11
    noting, 36
Social context, 9–10, 12
Social discourse, 84
Social issues, discursive research on, 46
Socially managed psychological concepts, 5

Social psychology, 46
Specificity, of research questions, 19–20
Speech
    direct vs. indirect, 91
    reported, 44, 91
Speech act theory, 10
Stake, management of, 90
Stakeholders, data analysis by, 63–64
Statistical generalizability, 72
Stiles, W., 73
Stokoe, E. H., 22–23
Stoppard, J. M., 21, 28, 72
Study design, 15–25
    archival document use in, 22–23
    framing research question in, 17–21
    initial literature searches in, 16–17
    new data generation in, 23–25
    opening statement of topic, 15–16
    and selecting data sources, 21–25
Subject, reconceptualization of, 83
Synthetic approach, 6

T

Talk, 9, 11, 21
Taylor, S., 83
Text, 11, 21
3-minute thesis, 72
Title, journal article, 68
Topic statement(s)
    changing, 17
    and framing of research question, 20, 21
    opening, 15–16

Tracy, S. J., 73, 79–80
Transcription(s)
    level of notational detail for, 32–33
    making, 32
    notations for, 32, 87
Transparency, 43, 74, 80
Tropes, 91

U

Underanalysis, avoiding, 40

V

Vagueness, details vs., 89
Valiakalayil, Agitha, 23
Validity, 73, 74
Variability, 28
"Variables," use of term, 71
Versions, 12

W

Wade, A., 55–56
Wetherell, M., 5, 74, 83–84
"What" research questions, 9, 17–19
WHO (World Health Organization), 28
"Why" research questions, 9, 19
Wiggins, S., 5, 6, 9, 37, 51, 56, 81
Willig, C., 9
Wood, L. A., 36, 37, 58, 74, 76
Words, research focusing on single, 45
World Health Organization (WHO), 28

About the Author

Linda M. McMullen, PhD, is professor emerita of psychology at the University of Saskatchewan (Canada). She is coauthor (with Frederick J. Wertz, Kathy Charmaz, Ruthellen Josselson, Rosemarie Anderson, and Emalinda McSpadden) of *Five Ways of Doing Qualitative Analysis: Phenomenological Psychology, Grounded Theory, Discourse Analysis, Narrative Research, and Intuitive Inquiry* and coeditor (with Janet M. Stoppard) of *Situating Sadness: Women and Depression in Social Context.* Her recent publications include discursive analyses of service providers' and service users' accounts of depression and the use of antidepressants. She has served as president of the Society for Qualitative Inquiry in Psychology (a section of the Division of Quantitative and Qualitative Methods of the American Psychological Association) and has been recognized by the Canadian Psychological Association (Fellow; Distinguished Member, Section for Women and Psychology), the Saskatchewan Psychological Association (Outstanding and Longstanding Service to the Profession), and the University of Saskatchewan Faculty Association (Academic Freedom Award).

About the Series Editors

Clara E. Hill, PhD, earned her doctorate at Southern Illinois University in 1974. She started her career in 1974 as an assistant professor in the Department of Psychology, University of Maryland, College Park, and is currently there as a professor.

She is currently the president-elect of the Society for the Advancement of Psychotherapy, and has been the president of the Society for Psychotherapy Research, the editor of the *Journal of Counseling Psychology*, and the editor of *Psychotherapy Research*.

Dr. Hill was awarded the Leona Tyler Award for Lifetime Achievement in Counseling Psychology from Division 17 (Society of Counseling Psychology) and the Distinguished Psychologist Award from Division 29 (Society for the Advancement of Psychotherapy) of the American Psychological Association, the Distinguished Research Career Award from the Society for Psychotherapy Research, and the Outstanding Lifetime Achievement Award from the Section on Counseling and Psychotherapy Process and Outcome Research of the Society for Counseling Psychology. Her major research interests are helping skills, psychotherapy process and outcome, training therapists, dream work, and qualitative research.

She has published more than 250 journal articles, 80 chapters in books, and 17 books (including *Therapist Techniques and Client Outcomes: Eight Cases of Brief Psychotherapy*; *Helping Skills: Facilitating Exploration, Insight, and Action*; and *Dream Work in Therapy: Facilitating Exploration, Insight, and Action*).

Sarah Knox, PhD, joined the faculty of Marquette University in 1999 and is a professor in the Department of Counselor Education and Counseling Psychology in the College of Education. She earned her doctorate at the University of Maryland and completed her predoctoral internship at The Ohio State University.

Dr. Knox's research has been published in a number of journals, including *The Counseling Psychologist*, *Counselling Psychology Quarterly*, *Journal of Counseling Psychology*, *Psychotherapy*, *Psychotherapy Research*, and *Training and Education in Professional Psychology*. Her publications focus on the psychotherapy process and relationship, supervision and training, and qualitative research. She has presented her research both nationally and internationally and has provided workshops on consensual qualitative research at both U.S. and international venues.

She currently serves as coeditor-in-chief of *Counselling Psychology Quarterly* and is also on the publication board of Division 29 (Society for the Advancement of Psychotherapy) of the American Psychological Association. Dr. Knox is a fellow of Division 17 (Society of Counseling Psychology) and Division 29 (Society for the Advancement of Psychotherapy) of the American Psychological Association.